HOUSTON IS COOKING

At Home

by Ann Criswell

Nutritionist
Linda McDonald, M.S., R.D., L.D.

Wine Consultant
Denman Moody

Editor
Ann Steiner

Foreword
Ron Stone

Publisher
Fran Fauntleroy

HG

HOUSTON
GOURMET

OUR SPECIAL THANKS TO

Ed Daniels - *Photography*

Mark Ruisinger - *Mark Anthony Florist - Flowers*

LeGraphics - *Graphic Design*

Nancy Hudgins - *Publicity*

Wetmore & Company - *Printing*

Events - *Table Appointments; China: Rosenthal - Versace*

Glazer's Distributors

Republic Beverage

Rice Epicurean Markets

Special Friends whose beautiful homes are showcased in our Chef's photos
Beverly Harris and Lovice Brown

Houston Gourmet
Houston, Texas

Copyright ©1998 by Houston Gourmet

Printed in the United States of America

ISBN 1-882296-04-4

Library of Congress Cataloging-In-Publication data
Houston Gourmet Publishing Company

All recipes are reprinted with permission of authors.
Photographs printed with permission of Ed Daniels.
LiteFare and nutritional information printed with permission of Linda McDonald.

FOREWORD BY RON STONE

I happened to be looking through a learned journal I keep on my coffee table to impress guests, and it contained an essay on food. One sentence jumped out at me. It said: "Barbecue is probably America's most overrated food!" It went on to suggest that the people who profess to like it probably aren't exposed to real cuisine.

Well, we should take up a collection, folks, and bring the fellow who wrote that down to Houston. The great diversity of the city and the food that is available would probably shake him to his very New England soul.

What a shock it would be to learn that Houstonians don't just eat barbecue or chicken fried steak and cream gravy with a side of fried okra; we often go for portobello mushrooms, hand-cut pasta, lamb chops and vegetables flambé. I could go on and on but I can't write the words "Grand Marnier Soufflé" without salivating.

In Houston, there are more fine restaurants and great chefs than the newcomer imagines or than the person who has lived here a while has had time to find. The food and cooking represent all that is traditional — and all that is new — plus some rather exciting stops in between.

My friend Ann Criswell knows them all. I have had to build out the kitchen at home so my wife Patsy can store all the recipes that Ann has published in the Houston Chronicle. Now this cookbook will take you further than you have ever gone without having to leave the comfort of your own kitchen.

As we approach the millennium, Houston is putting an exclamation point on the fact of life and business: "The Twentieth Century was THE century for Houston!" In the last hundred years we have gone from a sleepy little town to a dynamic city. The offshore oil industry is bigger than it has ever been. Billion-dollar deals are announced almost daily, it seems. We build computers; our port is bustling; and NASA is preparing for the 21st century in space.

If that is not exciting enough — well you get the message. All this hustle and bustle makes you hungry, doesn't it?

INTRODUCTION

ANN CRISWELL
Food Editor
The Houston Chronicle

Home cooking has come full circle. The chefs in this cookbook, our eighth, have reinvented their home food for the restaurants, and now they pass it on so you can adapt the recipes for your own home kitchen.

"Houston Is Cooking At Home" gives clues to how Houston restaurants are developing as we approach the millennium. Ingredients and techniques have changed tremendously since our first book 20 years ago. International travel,

affluence and increased leisure time have made consumers more knowledgeable. People have learned to appreciate American regional foods and acknowledge the job of chef as a profession. They also are more concerned about health and nutrition.

Meals are much less formal today; it's common to dress casually for all but black-tie events. There are fewer courses and rich sauces. Most sauces are a reduction of natural juices or stock, vegetables and perhaps wine; flour is seldom used as a thickener. Exotic vegetables, fruit, wild game and meats such as emu and ostrich have become common menu items.

Many of the chefs had humble beginnings and understand simple, everyday foods. But as professionals they have taken them to new heights. What a revelation to encounter mashed potatoes blended variously with roasted garlic, red wine reduction, three cheeses, exotic mushrooms or truffles and truffle oil.

With the incredible diversity in Houston restaurants in the past few years, we are treated to tastes of home from half a world away in Asia and Europe to Mexico and far-flung corners of our own country. Some examples: Alice Vongvisith of Nit Noi brings us exotic flavors from her home in Thailand, a center of rice noodle manufacturing where the family grew its own rice. Jim Mills of the Houstonian approaches rice from the perspective of growing up on the Texas Gulf Coast.

Carl Walker of Brennan's, who grew up on a farm in Missouri, turns humble oatmeal into a sophisticated dessert, Oatmeal Custard, that has become a best seller at Brennan's. Mark Cox of Mark's reflects his West Virginia background in the imaginative use of corn and other down-home southern vegetables. Gerard Brach bases the menus at Chez Nous on French classics from his homeland. But he also uses the classics as a springboard for nouveau creations that combine the best of yesterday with the best of today. That's why you will find Escargots de Bourgogne in herb butter co-existing on the menu with Smoked Scottish Salmon with Horseradish Cheesecake and Chive Emulsion.

Houstonians love to dine out, and do so at a rate higher than the national average. And when we go out to eat we are usually in the mood to celebrate; we're not counting calories and fat grams. In the signature restaurant dishes in this book you will see lots of cream and butter. But at home you can adapt the recipes to more everyday cooking by using the substitutes or controlling the portions as listed by nutritionist Linda McDonald.

People are still cooking at home, but today "preparing a meal" often means assembling items from take-out, prepared dishes from the supermarket and other home meal replacements. Catering has achieved new status also, and many of our finest food specialty stores provide catering-quality items or will cater the entire meal. What a boon for the holidays!

The Special Helps section at the back of the book includes cooking terms and descriptions of techniques — clarifying butter, making brown sauce and roux, deglazing a pan and other basic techniques.

You will notice that professionals think the quality and integrity of the ingredients are significant to the success of many dishes. In stocking your pantry and refrigerator, add their favorites to your shopping list — extra-virgin and pomace olive oil, balsamic vinegar, chilies, high-quality fresh and dried pasta, shallots, Roma tomatoes, black beans, exotic mushrooms, mascarpone and goat cheese, ginger, cilantro and field greens (various combinations of gourmet baby greens and lettuces).

The Shopping Guide lists sources for the ordinary and extraordinary ingredients called for in recipes.

We hope you will enjoy "Houston Is Cooking At Home" by experimenting with the recipes and techniques and inviting friends in to share.

TABLE OF CONTENTS

FOREWORD 5

INTRODUCTION 6

TABLE OF CONTENTS 8

ABOUT ANN CRISWELL.............................10

LINDA MCDONALD....................................11

DINING WITH WINE AT HOME......................12

ALDO'S 13
Bread Soup (Acquacotta alla Sienese)
Shrimp with Frangelico Sauce
Fillet of Snapper with Roasted Garlic Sauce
Lamb Shanks Osso Buco Style
The Southern Star — White or Dark Chocolate Cake

AMBASSADOR 17
Sautéed Shrimp with Hot Sauce
Chicken with Dry Red Peppers
Eggplant Szechwan Style
Braised Beef with Brown Sauce

ARCODORO 23
Field Greens and Artichoke Salad (Mista del Campo)
Steak of Gold (Costata d'Oro)
Pork Loin with Perfumes of the Forest
Tiramisu

BISTRO LANCASTER 27
Red Pepper Bisque with Lump Crabmeat & Tabbouleh
Grilled Pork Chops with Pecan Sauce
Mashed Sweet Potatoes with Roasted Garlic
Warm Croissant Bread Pudding

BRENNAN'S 33
Beef Debris Gumbo
Cornmeal Drop Biscuits
Root Vegetable Slaw with Ginger Vinaigrette
Oatmeal Custard
Chocolate Molten Soufflé with White Chocolate Sauce

CAFÉ NOCHE 37
Stuffed Mushroom Appetizer
   with White Wine Butter Sauce & Corn Relish
Green Enchiladas (Enchiladas Verdes)
Three Milk Cake (Pastel de Tres Leches)
Ceviche with Avocado Cream Sauce

CAVATORE 43
Fried Calamari (Fritti di Calamari)
Mussel Soup (Zuppa di Cozze)
Shrimp Giuliana (Scampi Giuliana)
Chicken Grogorio (Pollo alla Grogorio)
Veal Marsala
Fettuccine Roma

CHEZ NOUS...47
White Gazpacho
Roasted Flounder with Garlic & Bacon
Walnut Tart with Jack Daniel's Ice Cream
Vegetable Ragout with Chervil

CLIVE'S 53
Oven Baked Salmon on Rock Salt
Creamed Spinach
Sirloin and Ribeye Rub
Steak Cooking Tips
Dijon Vinaigrette
Sticky Toffee Cake with Caramel Sauce

DAMIAN'S 57
Thomas' Salad (Insalata Tomasso)
Stuffed Pork Loin (Lombo Porchetta Imbottire)
Dominic's Penne Pasta (Penne alla Dominic)
Marsala and Mascarpone Zabaglione with Strawberries

DEVILLE 61
Gougères
Texas Gulf Coast Lump Crab Cakes
   with Ginger Soy Butter
Roasted Sweet Garlic Whipped Potatoes
Tahitian Vanilla Fruit Soup

EMPRESS..65
Filet Mignon a la Empress
Steamed Salmon with Fresh Ginger and Scallions
Crispy Chicken with Ginger, Green Onion Sauce
Lemon Baked Cheesecake

GRILLE 5115 71
Goat Cheese Salad with Apple and
   Sun-Dried Tomato Vinaigrette
Salmon Risotto with Red Pepper Cream Sauce
Susan's Mother's Carrot Cake with Cream Cheese Frosting

TABLE OF CONTENTS

THE HOUSTONIAN 75
Southwest Caesar Salad
Jalapeño Barbequed Shrimp with Pico de Gallo Rice
Macadamia Nut Chocolate Caramel Torte

LA TOUR d'ARGENT 79
Lentil Soup
Shrimp Orzo Ferrari
Salmon de Coquina
Chicken Griselda
Roasted Duck with Cherry Sauce

MARK'S 83
Grilled Corn Chowder with Red Potatoes and Thyme
Corn Risotto
Twice Baked Potatoes
Molasses and Honey Roasted Pork Tenderloin
    with Caramelized Balsamic Vinegar Sauce

NIT NOI 89
Alice's Chicken Delight
Cabbage Soup
Crispy Red Snapper
Thai Sticky Rice with Thai Custard and Mango

POST OAK GRILL 93
Lamb Enchiladas
Corn Crusted Redfish with Cilantro Avocado Sauce
Baked Alaska

REDWOOD GRILL 97
Shelly's Salad
Chilled Jumbo Shrimp with Jalapeño Remoulade
Beer Cheese Soup
Jalapeño Corn Muffins
Mixed Berry Cobbler

RIVIERA GRILL 101
Stilton, Endive and Baby Field Greens
    with Spicy Walnuts & Walnut Vinaigrette
Seared Sea Scallops with Red Onion Marmalade
Grilled Angus Filet Mignon
    with Mushroom, Dried Cranberry Ragout
Scalloped Potatoes Riviera
Crème Brûlée Riviera

ROTISSERIE FOR BEEF AND BIRD 107
Mallard Duck with Black Walnuts
Venison Tenderloin with Bell Peppers
Upside-down Caramelized Apple Tart

SOLERO 111
Roasted Red Bell Pepper Soup
Snapper Escabeche
Charred Vegetable Plate
Shrimp Arturo (Scampi Arturo)
Ceviche Solero
Mango Mousse

ST. REGIS 115
Champagne Brie Soup en Croute
Herb Seared Axis Venison and Pinot Noir Sauce
Black Truffle Whipped Potatoes
White Chocolate Ice Cream Charlotte

RICE EPICUREAN MARKETS / EPICUREAN CATERING
COMPANY 119
Cedar Planked Salmon
    with Raspberry Chipotle Sauce
Southwestern Pasta Primavera
Grilled Shrimp with Tomato Jam
Honey Crimson Glazed Pork Tenderloin
    with Mixed Greens and Toasted Pecans
Texas Pecan Chocolate Bourbon Torte
    with Bourbon Crème Anglaise

FRAN FAUNTLEROY, ANN STEINER....................125

HEALTHY RECIPE MODIFICATIONS 126

SPECIAL HELPS 128

SHOPPING GUIDE 130

NUTRITIONAL ANALYSIS 134

INDEX 142

WHO'S WHO
    (KEY TO BACK COVER PHOTOGRAPH)

ORDER FORM

"Houston — This is the greatest city to call home — with all the diversity, all the activities from the Opera to the Rodeo to the Rockets, Houston doesn't miss a beat — The people are pleasant and friendly — the pace is fast — and the spirit and energy is unlike any other place we have ever known — the neighborhoods of the city are warm and welcoming, evoking an old-fashioned sense of friends & family."

Houston is a Great City, one we are glad to call home!

ABOUT ANN CRISWELL

Ann Criswell has been employed at the Houston Chronicle for 37 years and has been food editor since 1966. She has written freelance food articles, authored eight cookbooks and edited several others. As food editor of the Chronicle she contributed most of the recipes in the "Texas the Beautiful Cookbook" published in October 1986.

She is a member of the Association of Food Journalists, Houston Culinary Guild and Houston Culinary Historians.

In 1987, she was named the first honorary member of the South Texas Dietetic Association and received an award of excellence from the American Heart Association, American Cancer Society and Texas Restaurant Association. In 1992, the Texas Dietetic Association named her Media Person of the Year.

Scholarships have been given in her name to the Houston Community College and School of Culinary Arts at the Art Institute of Houston.

Because of a special interest in wine, she wrote a wine column for many years in the Chronicle and has made several wine tours in Europe and California. She also has judged Texas wine competitions and national cooking contests including the National Beef Cook-Off, Pillsbury BAKE-OFF and the National Chicken Cooking Contest.

Among her major interests are the End Hunger Network, Houston Food Bank and the annual Share our Strength Taste of the Nation benefit for anti-hunger projects.

She is an honor graduate of Texas Woman's University. Her late husband, Jim, was a Houston newspaperman. She has a daughter, Catherine; son, Charles; and four grandchildren, Ryan and Christopher Criswell and James and Ann Claire Lester.

LINDA MCDONALD, M.S., R.D., L.D.

Food is a personal and professional passion to Linda. As editor and publisher of "*Supermarket Savvy*", a bi-monthly newsletter for health professionals, Linda tracks the latest food trends and reports on new foods in the supermarket. Restaurants have also been a special interest since 1988 when she was honored by the American Heart Association for development of the first "Houston Area Dining Out Guide—Heart Healthy Houston."

Linda now serves on the board of the Houston Culinary Guild and is a member of the International Association of Culinary Professionals, Roundtable for Women in Foodservice, the American Dietetic Association and Les Dames d'Escoffier.

Linda's unique expertise has enhanced menus, food products, educational materials, health professional journals and newsletters. "Houston Is Cooking At Home" is the ninth book that has benefited from Linda's nutrition knowledge.

Linda McDonald, a food and nutrition consultant to the food industry, is dedicated to helping you enjoy food without any negative consequences. Her restaurant LiteFare tips as well as the Healthy Recipe Modification Tips and Recipe Nutritional Analysis in "Houston Is Cooking At Home" will give you the knowledge needed to make informed decisions about the food you eat.

She holds a Master's Degree from the University of Texas Graduate School of Biomedical Sciences and is an honor graduate of the University of Houston with a degree in Nutrition and Dietetics.

A past president of the South Texas Dietetic Association and Nutrition Entrepreneurs, a dietetic practice group of the American Dietetic Association, and past director of the Texas Dietetic Association Foundation,

Happily married for 37 years, Linda and John McDonald are parents of two grown, married children—Susan and Scott Sorensen and Scott and Melissa McDonald. Linda delights in being called "Mema" by three grandchildren—Alexis, Stephen and Julia Rose.

DINING WITH WINE AT HOME BY DENMAN MOODY 🍇

There is no question that properly matched wine and food taste significantly better than either can taste by itself.

Some people say that food and wine at dinner should only provide a backdrop for discussing the important issues of the day. This may be true at times. However, when a dinner is planned with complementary wines, it could be argued that no other topic need to be discussed except the food and the wines.

In enjoying the arts through the senses, the eyes alone are sometimes used — sometimes the eyes and ears. During a great meal, which one could liken to an evening of entertainment, one uses the eyes, ears, taste, smell and touch. And it doesn't have to be expensive.

For most recipes, there are two wines mentioned: the first being under $10 and the second between $10-$20. If there is a third wine, it is a great wine which would cost over $20.

To help with diversification and innovation, I sought and received the aid of two of the most respected and knowledgeable wine people anywhere: John Rydman and Bear Dalton at Spec's Liquors at 2410 Smith. The end product from the three of us, each coming from a different wine background, should open new vistas for all readers. If the exact wine mentioned is not available, ask for something similar (and similarly priced) and hopefully, it will work just as well.

Denman Moody, connoisseur and wine writer, was editor and publisher of "Moody's Wine Review," which the "Washington Post" said was the "...best publication in this country for tracking the state of rare and exotic wines."

Denman is a former Host of the Houston Chapter of the International Wine and Food Society, as well as Commander Emeritus of the Knights of the Vine. He is also Vice President of Amici della Vite and a member of the Commanderie de Bordeaux.

His wine articles have appeared in numerous publications including: "Revue du Vin de France," Paris; "International Wine and Food Society Journal," London; "International Wine Review;" "Wine and Spirits;" and "Texas Monthly."

In his spare time, Denman is a financial consultant.

🍇

ALDO'S

BREAD SOUP (ACQUACOTTA ALLA SIENESE)
SHRIMP WITH FRANGELICO SAUCE
FILLET OF SNAPPER WITH ROASTED GARLIC SAUCE
LAMB SHANKS OSSO BUCO STYLE
THE SOUTHERN STAR — WHITE OR DARK CHOCOLATE CAKE

Aldo ElSharif's background is a mixture of Egyptian, Italian, French, Greek, English and American. The result: the menu at Aldo's is a blend of handpicked ingredients and wines, classic cooking techniques and the latest from the world's markets. Some of the treasures: Tufino truffle cheese, white truffle oil and specialty pastas from Italy along with San Daniele prosciutto, which is aged 600 days, from Fruili; smoked eel from Holland; exotic mushrooms from Italy, Oregon and New York; Amish-bred chickens and turkeys from the Midwest; fish from world sources; and game and fresh herbs from Texas.

Aldo's
Dining con Amoré

Aldo lived in Egypt where his family worked for King Farouk. After Farouk was expelled from Egypt, the family moved to Aldo's mother's hometown of Catania, Italy, then to Lake Como. Aldo worked for a trattoria in Milan three years as an unpaid apprentice. At 19 he went to France and for the next six years traveled and worked in Europe. At 26 he came to New York to join his brother and worked at the Russian Tea Room and the Waldorf Astoria.

Ready for a new experience, he came to Houston and worked at Buttarazzi's on FM 1960 West, where his cooking quickly won acclaim. Moving on, he opened Aldo's in December 1995, in an old two-story wood-frame house on lower Westheimer. It now offers the welcome of a comfortable home with hunter green walls and carpeting, cream-colored box ceilings, fireplaces, roomy chairs and antiques in an atmosphere that encourages guests to relax and dine leisurely.

Because there are less than a dozen tables, guests often feel they have been invited to a private dinner party with Aldo as host, maitre d' and cook. That's the impression Aldo encourages as he moves from table to table suggesting a special dish and slipping back and forth to the kitchen to oversee the cooking or perhaps to put the finishing touches on a signature sauce. Guests are quickly aware that here is someone who loves to cook. More than 80 percent of the menu is homey and traditional, says Aldo who practices a "look to the 'fridge" philosophy of creativity.

An award-winning wine list of more than 800 selections often is the inspiration for wine dinners in an upstairs party room that accommodates 60. For these functions, the restaurant is closed to regular clients.

Aldo also is opening Aldo's Wine Bar downtown at 301 Main Street. It will feature wines and appetizers and light fare such as brick-oven baked pizzas and wild game salami.

—————————— *LITE FARE* ——————————

Chef Aldo runs a personalized restaurant where taste and texture are supreme. Fresh herbs and vegetables compliment the pasta, lean meat and seafood dishes. Enjoy the special spreads, which are one-third butter and two-thirds egg white, on a slice of crusty bread. Special requests are encouraged so ask for grilled entrées with no or little added oil.

Aldo's
219 Westheimer
Houston, Tx 77006
713-523-2536

BREAD SOUP (ACQUACOTTA ALLA SIENESE)

4	tablespoons extra-virgin olive oil
1/2	yellow onion, chopped
1	tablespoon chopped garlic
1/4	pound prosciutto skin or fat*
1	(19-ounce) can cannellini beans (Italian white kidney beans)
1	cup tomato sauce (8-ounce can)
4	cups chicken broth
1	tablespoon chopped fresh Italian parsley
10	fresh sage leaves
	Salt and freshly ground black pepper to taste
4	(1-inch) slices Italian bread
	Extra-virgin olive oil
	Pesto

Heat oil in heavy stockpot. Sauté onion and garlic with prosciutto skin until slightly golden. Add beans including liquid, tomato sauce, broth, parsley and sage. Season with salt and pepper. Bring to a boil, reduce heat and simmer 10 minutes. Occasionally skim foam from top until no foam appears. Brush bread with oil and pesto; grill, broil or toast. Pour soup into 4 bowls; garnish each serving with toasted bread slice. Serves 4.

 To reduce sodium, use low-sodium chicken broth, low-sodium tomato sauce and eliminate added salt. Reduce oil for sautéing to 1 tablespoon. Eliminate oil for bread slices and brush with a small amount of pesto.

Michele Chiarlo Barbera d'Asti (Italy) or Beyerskloof Pinotage (South Africa); Pellegrini Barbera (Italy).

Usually trimmed by the butcher. Ask for it at the meat counter. If not available, use prosciutto. Aldo's uses San Daniele, a premium prosciutto from Fruili, which is aged 600 days.

SHRIMP WITH FRANGELICO SAUCE

3/4	cup pure olive oil
8	jumbo shrimp (Spanish if possible), peeled leaving tails intact
1/2	cup all-purpose flour
1	tablespoon chopped shallots
1/2	cup Frangelico (hazelnut liqueur)
	Juice of 1 1/2 key limes
1/2	cup whipping cream
1	tablespoon unsalted butter
1/2	cup fish stock
1/4	cup golden raisins
1/4	cup julienned dried apricots
1	tablespoon chopped fresh Italian parsley
	Salt and freshly ground black pepper to taste
	Lump crabmeat or crawfish tails (optional)

Heat oil in heavy skillet. Dust shrimp in flour and sauté lightly on both sides. Remove from pan, set aside and keep warm. Drain oil. Pour shallots, Frangelico, lime juice, cream and butter into skillet. Stir in stock, raisins, apricots and parsley. Simmer 5 minutes, or until reduced by half. Season with salt and pepper. Add crabmeat if desired. Arrange 2 shrimp on each plate and pour sauce over top. Serves 4.

Reduce oil to 1/4 cup and substitute half-and-half for cream.

Ehses Hansen Wehlener Klosterberg QbA (Germany); Trimbach Riesling (France).

FILLET OF SNAPPER WITH ROASTED GARLIC SAUCE

1/2	cup pure olive oil
4	(6-to-8-ounce) snapper fillets
1/4	cup all-purpose flour
1	tablespoon unsalted butter
1/2	tablespoon chopped shallots
1/2	cup fish stock
1/2	cup dry white wine
1/4	cup whipping cream
2	heads garlic, roasted and removed from papery skin
1	tablespoon chopped fresh Italian parsley
10 to 15	leaves fresh basil, halved Lump crabmeat, shrimp, scallops or crawfish tails (optional)

Heat oil in heavy skillet. Dust fillets with flour; shake off excess. Lightly sauté fillets. Remove from pan, set aside and keep warm. Drain oil and melt butter in same skillet; sauté shallots 1 minute. Add stock, wine, cream, garlic, parsley and basil. Simmer over medium heat 5 to 10 minutes, or until sauce is reduced by half. Add crabmeat if desired. Place 1 fillet on each plate and pour sauce over top. Serve with sautéed vegetables and potatoes. Serves 4.

🍎 Reduce oil to 2 tablespoons and substitute half-and-half for cream. Limit snapper to 6-ounce fillets.

🍇 St. Francis Chardonnay, Iron Horse Fume-Blanc or St. Supery Sauvignon-Blanc or St. Supery Chardonnay; Murphy-Goode Fume-Blanc Reserve or De Loach Chardonnay O.F.S.

LAMB SHANKS OSSO BUCO STYLE

1/2	cup pure olive oil
4	large American lamb shanks (about 3/4 pound each)
1/2	cup all-purpose flour
4	large carrots, chopped
4	whole heads garlic, coarsely chopped
3	large onions, chopped
1	stalk (whole head) celery with leaves, chopped
2	cups whole plum Italian tomatoes
1/4	cup fresh rosemary sprigs
1/8	cup fresh thyme sprigs
1/8	cup fresh sage leaves
4	cups veal or beef stock
1 1/2	cups dry white wine
1 1/2	cups sherry
	Salt and freshly ground black pepper to taste

Heat oil in heavy skillet. Dust shanks with flour and sear quickly on all sides until dark brown.

In large heavy stockpot, add carrots, garlic, onion, celery, tomatoes, rosemary, thyme, sage, stock, wine, sherry, salt and pepper along with browned shanks. Cover and simmer 1 1/2 hours over low heat. Remove shanks; strain stock for sauce. Pour sauce over lamb shanks and serve with risotto, pasta or polenta. Serves 4.

🍎 Lamb is a high-fat meat. Reduce oil to 2 tablespoons. Serve with a low-fat or fat-free starch such as rice or pasta.

🍇 Cerretto Zonchera Barolo (Italy); Il Fratello Caugamonga Zinfandel (Italy); Bruno Giacosa Barbaresco or Angelo Gaja Barbaresco (Italy).

THE SOUTHERN STAR
WHITE OR DARK CHOCOLATE CAKE

20 ounces white or dark high-quality chocolate, such as Callebaut
11 eggs, separated
1/2 cup plus 2 tablespoons unsalted butter, clarified (see Special Helps section)
1/2 cup sugar
1 pound mascarpone cheese, softened
1/2 cup all-purpose flour
   Pinch of salt
2 cups Frangelico (hazelnut liqueur)
1/2 cup julienned dried apricots
1/2 cup golden raisins
1/2 cup chopped nuts of choice
   Southern Star Sauce, optional (recipe follows)

Preheat oven to 350 degrees. Cut chocolate into pieces. Melt chocolate in top of double boiler or in microwave (see Special Helps section); set aside. Beat egg whites with wire whip until stiff peaks are formed; reserve.

Cream butter and sugar in electric mixer bowl. Add egg yolks, mascarpone, flour, salt and Frangelico; blend thoroughly. Stir in apricots, raisins and nuts. Fold in egg whites. Pour into well-greased 10-inch springform pan. Bake 1 hour until cake puffs up and is firm to the touch. Remove from oven and cool on counter. When cool, remove from pan. To serve, slice and rewarm each piece in oven until soft. Serve with Southern Star Sauce if desired. Serves 12 to 16.

Note: At Aldo's, sometimes a slice of each — dark and white — cake is served.

SOUTHERN STAR SAUCE

1 cup white or dark chocolate, such as Callebaut, melted
1/2 cup whipping cream
1/2 cup Frangelico (hazelnut liqueur)
1/2 pound mascarpone cheese, softened
1/4 cup chopped dried fruit (figs, apricots or raisins as desired)
1/4 cup chopped nuts

Southern Star Sauce

Combine chocolate, cream, Frangelico, mascarpone, fruit and nuts in saucepan and bring to a boil. Serve hot over cake. Makes about 3 1/2 cups.

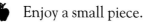 Enjoy a small piece.

Marrietta Cuvée Angeli; Queen Adelaide Tawny Port (Australia).

SAUTÉED SHRIMP WITH HOT SAUCE
CHICKEN WITH DRY RED PEPPERS
EGGPLANT SZECHWAN STYLE
BRAISED BEEF WITH BROWN SAUCE

Many customers have grown up with Ambassador Chinese Restaurant, which opened in 1976. Known primarily for Cantonese cuisine and friendly service, Ambassador has added spicier Hunan-style dishes during the past 22 years. But owners Wendy and Henry Wang know that treasured favorites such as Egg Rolls (still made by hand), Moo Goo Gai Pan, Won Ton Soup, Pepper Steak and Chicken Chow Mein deserve permanent status on the menu.

AMBASSADOR

Wendy describes herself as "Overseas Chinese" because she lived in Japan and Korea before moving to Houston in 1972. Her family was in the restaurant business in Korea and Taiwan. She was a teacher in Korea, and although she has always loved to cook, she mainly does so only at home now.

She and Henry met in Japan. Wendy worked in a friend's restaurant after moving here. She and Henry opened Ambassador a year and a half later. Wendy is the creative force behind the menu and Henry oversees the restaurant kitchen. Wendy knows most customers by name, and their loyalty can be attributed as much to her friendly hospitality as to the food.

"People know more about Chinese food now than when we first opened, and we've added a lot of spicy food. I love to watch people eat my food and enjoy it."

Hot, spicy dishes are indicated by pepper symbols on the menu. They include such favorites as Hot and Sour Soup, Mandarin Beef, Orange Beef, Kung Pao Chicken, Szechuan Shredded Chicken, Garlic Shrimp, Hot Braised Fish and Twice Cooked Pork.

The menu also includes several diet dishes and Special Salad, a signature dish. A mixture of sliced vegetables, shrimp, pork and chicken with a special sauce, it is popular anytime for light dining, but is especially refreshing in hot weather.

Family combination dinners are a good choice for groups; each menu can be expanded to serve more people by adding extra dishes. All come with egg rolls and fried rice.

The dining room seats 80 and its quiet ambiance encourages conversation and leisurely dining. Distinctive red silk lanterns, red covers over white tablecloths, silk flower arrangements, plants and lacquer screens give the room a comfortable, relaxed feel.

LITE FARE

The Ambassador menu has all the basics for healthy dining—lean meats, fresh vegetables and rice. Good choices are Steamed Vegetable Dumplings, Special Salad, steamed Diet Dishes, Hunan Chicken or Black Pepper Shrimp. Since most dishes are prepared when ordered, special requests can be honored. Request stir-fried in broth or with a minimum of oil.

Ambassador
4326 Richmond Ave.
Houston, Tx 77027
713-877-9394

SAUTÉED SHRIMP WITH HOT SAUCE

1	pound (16/20 count) shrimp, peeled and deveined
1	egg white
1	teaspoon wine
1 1/2	tablespoons cornstarch
1 1/2	teaspoons salt, divided
4	cups water
1	tablespoon vegetable oil
2	tablespoons chopped green onion
1	tablespoon chopped ginger
2	tablespoons tomato ketchup
4 to 5	dried hot red peppers
3	tablespoons chicken broth
1/2	teaspoon sugar
2	teaspoons cornstarch dissolved in 1 tablespoon water
1	teaspoon sesame oil

Clean and dry shrimp. Combine egg white, wine, cornstarch and 1 teaspoon salt in medium bowl; marinate shrimp in mixture at least 1/2 hour (longer is better).

Heat water to boiling in wok or deep pan. Cook shrimp until it starts to turn opaque, about 90 percent done; remove shrimp and drain water from pan.

Heat oil in same wok or pan; stir-fry onion and ginger. Add ketchup and peppers; stir quickly. Add broth, remaining 1/2 teaspoon salt and sugar; boil for only a few seconds. Then add cornstarch paste; stir until thickened. Sprinkle sesame oil over top. Serve with rice. Serves 4.

This dish is low in fat. Reduce sodium by using low-sodium chicken broth and eliminating added salt.

Franz Rem Bernkasteler Kurfurstlay Spätlese (Germany); Basserman Jordan Forster Jesuitgarten Spätlese (Germany).

CHICKEN WITH DRY RED PEPPERS

1	pound boneless, skinless chicken breasts
3	tablespoons lite soy sauce, divided
1 1/2	tablespoons cornstarch
5	cups water
8	pieces dried red pepper (each piece about 3 inches in length)
1	tablespoon vegetable oil
1	teaspoon chopped ginger
1	teaspoon Chinese chili paste (such as Sambal Oelek)
1	tablespoon white wine
1	tablespoon sugar
1	teaspoon cornstarch
1/2	teaspoon salt
1	teaspoon sesame oil

Cut chicken into 1-inch cubes. Combine 1 tablespoon soy sauce and 1 1/2 tablespoons cornstarch in a medium bowl. Marinate chicken cubes in mixture 10 minutes.

Heat water in large skillet or wok until boiling; add chicken and cook 2 minutes. Remove chicken and drain water.

Remove tips and seeds of red peppers; cut into 1-inch pieces; reserve. Heat oil in same skillet to fry dried red peppers until blackened. Add ginger, chili paste and chicken; stir quickly. Add remaining 2 tablespoons soy sauce; wine, sugar, 1 teaspoon cornstarch, salt and sesame oil; stir until thickened. Serves 4.

 This low-fat dish is a great source of vitamins A and C. Reduce sodium by using low-sodium soy sauce and eliminate added salt.

Messina Hof Riesling (Texas); Pike's Riesling (Australia).

EGGPLANT SZECHWAN STYLE

4	(12-ounce) firm Chinese eggplants, about 3 pounds
6	tablespoons water
1	tablespoon Chinese chili paste (such as Sambal Oelek)
1/2	tablespoon chopped ginger
1	teaspoon chopped garlic
2	tablespoons lite soy sauce
1	teaspoon sugar
1/2	teaspoon salt
1/2	cup chicken broth
1/2	tablespoon white vinegar
1/2	tablespoon sesame oil
1	tablespoon chopped green onion

Do not remove peel from eggplants but remove stem. Cut each eggplant into 4 lengthwise strips, then cut each strip in half yielding 8 pieces per eggplant.

Heat water to boiling in medium skillet. Add eggplant, reduce heat and cook until soft, about 3 minutes. Remove eggplant from skillet; set aside.

In same skillet, add chili paste, ginger and garlic; stir a few seconds. Add soy sauce, sugar, salt and broth; bring to a boil. Add reserved eggplant, cook about 1 minute, or until liquid is evaporated.

Add vinegar and sesame oil; stir until heated through. Sprinkle with onion to serve. Serves 4.

 This is a great low-fat recipe. Reduce sodium by using low-sodium soy sauce and chicken broth; eliminate added salt.

 Sonoma Creek Pinot Noir; Benziger Pinot Noir or Dehlinger Pinot Noir.

BRAISED BEEF WITH BROWN SAUCE

1 1/4	pounds beef (brisket or flank steak)
1	egg white, beaten
1/2	tablespoon cornstarch
1	teaspoon lite soy sauce (such as Kikkoman)
1/4	teaspoon freshly ground black pepper
8	cups boiling water
1	tablespoon sugar
1	tablespoon oil
3	green onions, sliced
5	slices ginger
2/3	cup lite soy sauce
1	tablespoon red wine
3	star anise

Cut beef into 1x1 1/2x1/2-inch pieces. Combine egg white, cornstarch, 1 teaspoon soy sauce and pepper in medium bowl. Marinate beef in mixture 5 to 10 minutes. Add beef to boiling water in large stockpot; cook 2 minutes. Drain beef and reserve stock to make soup (see Note below).

Put sugar and oil in wok and cook together until sugar is browned — don't let it burn. Add onion, ginger, 2/3 cup soy sauce, wine, star anise and beef to wok; stir-fry 2 minutes. Beef should be soft and juices reduced to 1/4 cup. Remove to plate with juices and accompany with rice. Serves 4.

Note: For soup, add 2 to 3 teaspoons salt and 1/2 teaspoon white pepper to leftover stock. Add chopped vegetables, such as green and white bok choy, celery and sauce-cooked noodles. Let simmer until hot then add a little sesame oil and chopped green onions.

Substitute flank steak for beef brisket. Eliminate oil and stir-fry in broth or a spray oil. Use low-sodium soy sauce. Serve with plain rice.

Domaine L'Espigouette Côtes du Rhone (France); Marrietta Syrah; Guigal Côte-Rôtie (France).

FACING PAGE, FROM LEFT: *Aldo ElSharif, Aldo's; Denman Moody, Wine Connoisseur; Wendy Wang, Ambassador.*

FOLLOWING PAGE, FROM LEFT: *Tommaso Lestinge, Efisio Farris, Arcodoro.*

FIELD GREENS AND ARTICHOKE SALAD (MISTA DEL CAMPO)
STEAK OF GOLD (COSTATA D'ORO)
PORK LOIN WITH PERFUMES OF THE FOREST (LONZA DI MAIALE AL PROFUMI DI BOSCO)
TIRAMISU

If you've never been to Sardinia, Italy, a visit to Arcodoro in the Centre at Post Oak is the next best thing. Owner Efisio Farris has re-created a little corner of his homeland with granite and marble tiles imported from quarries where his father and uncle once worked. Farris brought his high-school art teacher, Alfonso Silba, from Sardinia to do the wall murals and paintings depicting Sardinian scenes.

There's a menu item and setting for every taste and occasion from pizza baked in the wood-burning oven to sophisticated multi-course wine dinners. For casual dining, Farris and his wife Lori designed a bar and grillroom and adjacent outdoor patio. A state-of-the-art, high ventilation cigar room attracts those who enjoy a cigar and glass of port.

Menus feature the finest meats, fresh fish and seafood, cheeses, fresh herbs, breads and desserts. Arcodoro customers are treated to many items seldom or never served here before. Fresh buffalo mozzarella is flown in weekly from Italy.

Arcodoro has offered many customers their first taste of hand-rolled Sardinian teardrop pasta with forked grooves called Malloreddus, Risotto Nero (Arborio rice risotto with baby squid and squid ink), and bresaola (Italian sun-cured beef).

Farris buys fish directly from fish markets or off the boats docked at Kemah and Galveston two or three times a week. Some loyal customers come in every week for the whole fish baked in the wood-burning oven. It also is a preferred entrée at celebratory dinners.

Efisio, ever the perfectionist, plans the menus himself, choosing just the right preparation technique, side dishes and wine for the occasion. He might dress the fish simply with olive oil, balsamic vinegar, fresh vegetables and herbs or encase the fish in a kosher salt crust and roast it in the wood-burning oven.

Displays of fresh fish, vegetables and breads give diners a preview of the day's "catch." Breads are special at Arcodoro. Pane Carasau is one of the most popular — it is known as music bread because its papery leaves make a tinkling sound as they shatter.

The Farrises also own Pomodoro restaurant in Dallas. Both Arcodoro and Pomodoro were named among the 10 finest Italian restaurants in the country by Decanter magazine in 1997. They were the only two restaurants in Texas selected.

LITE FARE

Arcodoro uses a wood-burning oven for low-fat preparation, especially delicious with fish. Look on the menu for low-fat sauces called broths and salsas. If you are not sure about the fat content of a sauce, ask for it to be served on the side. Healthiest entrée is the whole-wheat fettuccini with roasted fresh vegetables.

*Arcodoro
5000 Westheimer
Houston, Tx 77056
713-621-6888*

FIELD GREENS AND ARTICHOKE SALAD (MISTA DEL CAMPO)

26 sprigs arugula, washed and trimmed, divided
2 raw artichoke hearts, thinly sliced
16 cherry tomatoes, quartered
1/2 cup toasted pine nuts
Vinaigrette (recipe follows)
1/4 cup freshly shredded Parmesan cheese*

*Shred Parmesan on large side of grater.

VINAIGRETTE

Juice of 2 lemons
1/2 cup extra-virgin olive oil
1 tablespoon balsamic vinegar
Salt and freshly ground black and red peppers to taste

Place 4 sprigs arugula on each of 4 plates. Chop remaining 10 sprigs arugula; toss with artichoke slices and tomatoes in medium bowl. Divide mixture and place on top of arugula. Sprinkle with pine nuts and drizzle Vinaigrette over salad. Top with Parmesan. Serve immediately. Serves 4.

Vinaigrette

Combine lemon juice, oil, vinegar, salt and peppers in small bowl with a whisk.

 Limit Vinaigrette to 1 tablespoon per serving. Reduce pine nuts and Parmesan to 2 tablespoons each.

Enjoy without wine.

STEAK OF GOLD (COSTATA D'ORO)

1 (25-ounce) bottle balsamic vinegar
Juice of 2 lemons and 1 lime
12 garlic cloves, chopped
4 sprigs fresh rosemary, broken up
4 (16-ounce) aged Black Angus ribeye steaks, cut about 1 1/2 inches thick
1 cup full-bodied red wine (such as Cannonau from Sardinia)
1 tablespoon cracked black pepper
1/4 cup extra-virgin olive oil
Salt (optional)

Combine vinegar, lemon juice, lime juice, garlic and rosemary as a marinade. Place steaks in mixture, cover and marinate in refrigerator 4 hours, making sure steaks are covered with liquid. Remove from marinade and grill as desired.

Add wine and pepper to marinade in saucepan and cook over low heat until slightly reduced, about 10 to 15 minutes. Use reduction as a sauce. Drizzle steaks with oil and sprinkle with salt if desired. Serves 4.

 Although red meat is a good source of iron, choose lean cuts (beef tenderloin) and limit portion size to 6 ounces, which contains 30% of the recommended daily intake for iron. Eliminate oil for drizzling.

Cannonau Riserva Sella e Mosca; Cabernet Sauvignon Marchese di Villa Marina Sella e Mosca.

PORK LOIN WITH PERFUMES OF THE FOREST
(LONZA DI MAIALE AL PROFUMI DI BOSCO)

1 (3-pound) boneless pork tenderloin
1/2 cup coarsely chopped dried apricots
1/2 cup coarsely chopped dried prunes
1/2 cup coarsely chopped dried apples
1/4 cup coarsely chopped dried banana chips
1/4 cup raisins
1/4 cup chopped pistachios
5 sprigs mint, chopped (optional)
Extra-virgin olive oil
Salt and freshly ground black pepper to taste
Tarragon Blueberry Sauce (recipe follows)
Fresh herbs for garnish (thyme and rosemary sprigs)

Preheat oven to 350 degrees. Clean and trim pork loin. Cut loin lengthwise but not all the way through; open up. Repeat procedure until loin is rolled out flat. Pound lightly with a meat mallet until uniformly flattened; blot dry. Toss apricots, prunes, apples, banana chips, raisins and pistachios in a medium bowl. Spread evenly over pork; sprinkle mint on top. Roll pork loin lengthwise (jellyroll fashion) and secure with kitchen twine. Transfer to a roasting pan and rub with oil, salt and pepper. Roast 40 to 50 minutes, or until meat thermometer inserted in center registers 160 degrees.

Prepare Tarragon Blueberry Sauce. Slice pork into 1/2-inch medallions. Fan medallions out on plate, pour Tarragon Blueberry Sauce over top and garnish with herb sprigs. Or, serve sauce separately. Serves 6 to 8.

Note: At Arcodoro this is roasted in a wood-burning oven.

TARRAGON BLUEBERRY SAUCE

1/4 cup extra-virgin olive oil
1 teaspoon chopped fresh tarragon
1 pint blueberries, washed and drained
1/4 cup Pernod
Pinch of sugar
Pinch of salt
1 cup vegetable broth

Tarragon Blueberry Sauce

Heat oil in saucepan. Add tarragon and blueberries; stir over medium heat until blueberries are softened. Pour in Pernod. Flambé, lighting carefully with a taper match. Add sugar and salt. Stir in broth and simmer 10 minutes, until thickened and smooth. Makes 2 cups.

Pork tenderloin is a lean cut of meat. Limit oil to 1 tablespoon. This recipe could serve 8 adequately.

Monica di Sardegna Perdera Argiolas; Montepulciano Riserva Zanna Dino Illuminati.

TIRAMISU

1	cup whipping cream (chill cream, bowl and beaters well)
1/2	cup powdered sugar
1/2	pound mascarpone cheese, softened
2	tablespoons sweet Italian Marsala wine
3	cups cold brewed Italian espresso
1/4	cup Kahlua liqueur
1/4	cup white rum
48	imported Italian ladyfingers (savoiardi)
	Bittersweet cocoa powder for garnish
	Berries, melon slices, lemon curls and mint leaves for garnish

With electric mixer whip cream adding sugar gradually. Fold in mascarpone with a spatula; stir in Marsala. Combine espresso with Kahlua and rum in another bowl. Arrange half the ladyfingers on a large serving plate and lightly coat with espresso mixture. Add another layer of ladyfingers, top with the whipped cream-mascarpone cream mixture.

Cover and refrigerate until firm, about 4 hours. Before serving, sprinkle with cocoa powder. Slice and serve on plates garnished with berries or a slice of melon, lemon curls and a mint leaf. Serves 6.

 Enjoy in moderation. Share with a friend.

Frangelico Hazelnut Liqueur (Italy); Antinori Vin Santo (Italy).

RED PEPPER BISQUE WITH LUMP CRABMEAT *& Tabbouleh*
GRILLED PORK CHOPS *with Pecan Sauce*
MASHED SWEET POTATOES WITH ROASTED GARLIC
WARM CROISSANT BREAD PUDDING

Louis Cressy, executive chef of Bistro Lancaster at The Lancaster Hotel, has been interested in cooking since he was a boy. For two years, from 10 to 12, with the help of his Cajun grandmother he tried to master the classic pâté feuilletée. After many attempts using margarine, they discovered that the secret to the puff pastry was using real butter.

"My grandmother instilled in me a love of and curiosity about cooking. I am pretty much convinced that no professional chef can compete with a grandmother's cooking."

The lesson of using the right ingredients and perseverance served him well in later years as he worked his way through the kitchens of some of New Orleans' finest hotels and two of the Brennan family establishments, Ristorante Bacco and Mr. B's.

"My style of cooking blends my Creole-Cajun youth with my classical French training. When creating a dish I like to chase the flavors that are already in foods naturally. I build on these and from that point, I find that if you pay attention, the dish will almost tell you what comes next." Cressy continues to experiment and perfect his style of Gulf Coast cooking, a melange of Creole, Cajun, Southern and south-of-the-Border. Consider Muffuletta Quesadillas and Tequila Smoked Salmon, Potato and Goat Cheese Terrine.

In 1993, he joined The Lancaster, a 93-room hotel in the downtown theater district. A property of Small Luxury Hotels, the hotel has genteel British ambiance that has attracted locals and travelers for 15 years. The hotel exudes the charm of an English country manor. The dining room has a clubby atmosphere created by polished hardwood floors, hunter green walls and framed hunting and botanical prints. Although the kitchen is responsible for breakfast, lunch, dinner, 24-hour room service and catering, it is astonishingly small. But it doesn't cramp

Cressy's style. Rather than elaborate sauces and garnishes, he sticks to classic techniques with flavor innovations such as Osso Bucco made with venison and served with Jalapeño Spaetzle and Fried Cactus Leaves.

One specialty is an Open-Face Tuna Sandwich made with fresh tuna, crushed tomatoes, basil and garlic with arugula and sweet potato chips. Red Pepper Bisque, Jumbo Lump Crab Cakes, Bourbon Pecan Pie with Orange Anglaise and Warm Croissant Bread Pudding are other menu jewels.

--- *LITE FARE* ---

Since this restaurant is an integral part of a luxury hotel, accommodating special requests for health or other reasons is not a problem. Although not always on the menu, a vegetarian entrée can be requested. Fish can be grilled with little or no added fat; dressings and sauces can be served on the side.

Bistro Lancaster
Lancaster Hotel
701 Texas Ave.
Houston, Tx 77002
713-228-9502

RED PEPPER BISQUE WITH LUMP CRABMEAT *& Tabbouleh*

Tabbouleh (recipe follows)
3   red bell peppers, stemmed, seeded and cut into chunks
1/2   cup diced fennel bulb
1/2   cup diced yellow onion
4   cups chicken broth, divided
1/3   cup melted butter
1/3   cup all-purpose flour
1/2   teaspoon salt, or to taste
      Freshly ground white pepper and cayenne pepper to taste
3   drops hot red pepper sauce
      Lump crabmeat, cleaned and picked over for garnish

Prepare Tabbouleh. Cook bell peppers, fennel, onion and 1 cup broth in large saucepan. When cooked down, add remaining 3 cups broth and bring to a boil. Whisk butter and flour together for a roux; add to broth. Reduce heat and simmer 45 minutes. Season with salt, pepper, cayenne and hot sauce. Puree in blender in batches; strain through a fine strainer before serving. Garnish with crabmeat and Tabbouleh. Serves 6.

TABBOULEH

3/4   cup bulghur
1 1/2   cups cold water
1/2   white onion, diced
1/2   bunch parsley (leaves only), chopped
1   garlic clove, minced
1   tablespoon olive oil
2   tomatoes, seeded and diced
4   fresh mint leaves, minced
      Juice of 1 lime
      Salt and freshly ground black pepper to taste

Tabbouleh

Soak bulghur in water 1 hour. Squeeze well to remove excess water. Mix in a medium bowl with onion, parsley, garlic, oil, tomatoes, mint leaves, lime juice, salt and pepper. Makes 1 1/2 cups.

Eliminate oil in Tabbouleh. In bisque, substitute low-sodium chicken broth for regular. Reduce butter to 2 tablespoons. Eliminate salt.

Savory & James Amontillado Sherry (Spain); Sandeman Royal Corregidor Sherry (Spain).

GRILLED PORK CHOPS *with Pecan Sauce*

1 1/2	cups Pecan Sauce (recipe follows)
6	(8-ounce) pork chops
1/4	cup olive oil
	Salt and freshly ground black pepper to taste

PECAN SAUCE

1	tablespoon butter
2	garlic cloves, crushed
2	sage leaves
2	shallots, diced
3	tablespoons flour
1/4	cup Calvados (applejack brandy)
2	cups chicken broth
1 1/2	teaspoons salt
3/4	teaspoon freshly ground white pepper
	Pinch of cayenne pepper
2	teaspoons maple syrup
1	tablespoon whipping cream
1/2	cup chopped pecans

Prepare Pecan Sauce. Coat chops with oil; season with salt and pepper. Place on grill and cook medium well done. To serve, top with Pecan Sauce. Accompany with Mashed Sweet Potatoes with Roasted Garlic and steamed asparagus. Serves 6.

Pecan Sauce

Heat butter in a medium saucepan; add garlic, sage leaves and shallots. Cook until translucent. Add flour and stir to form a paste. Pour in Calvados and broth; bring to a boil and simmer 30 minutes. Season with salt, pepper, cayenne and syrup. Adjust seasoning. Add cream. Strain through a fine strainer and add pecans. Cover and refrigerate extra sauce for future use. Makes 2 1/2 cups.

Pecan Sauce: Use low-sodium chicken broth. Cut pecans to 1/4 cup. Purchase 6-ounce pork chops. Eliminate oil to coat chops.

Benzier Carneros Chardonnay; Mac Rostie Carneros Chardonnay (White) or Nalle or Titus Zinfandel (Red).

MASHED SWEET POTATOES WITH ROASTED GARLIC

3	large sweet potatoes
10	garlic cloves
3	tablespoons olive oil
2	teaspoons salt
1	teaspoon freshly ground black pepper
3	tablespoons unsalted butter

Peel potatoes and place in a medium saucepan; cover with water. Boil until tender; drain. Meanwhile, preheat oven to 350 degrees. Place garlic in an ovenproof pan, drizzle with oil and roast 10 minutes, or until brown. Combine potatoes and garlic in a food processor and process until smooth. Add salt, pepper and butter; mix again. Adjust seasoning. Serves 6.

Sweet potatoes are a good source of vitamin A. Reduce oil and butter to 1 tablespoon each. Eliminate salt.

WARM CROISSANT BREAD PUDDING

8 egg yolks
1 whole egg
1 3/4 cups sugar
1 tablespoon vanilla extract
1 3/4 teaspoons salt
3/4 cup milk
3 cups whipping cream
9 large croissants, torn into pieces
Mulled Sultanas (recipe follows)
2 cups Rum Vanilla Bean Caramel Sauce (recipe follows)

MULLED SULTANAS

1/2 cup dried cranberries
1/2 cup raisins
1/2 cup golden raisins
1/2 cup sugar
1/4 cup rum
1 teaspoon ground cinnamon
1/2 teaspoon ground cloves
1/4 teaspoon ground nutmeg
Water

RUM VANILLA BEAN CARAMEL SAUCE

1/2 cup water
2 cups sugar
1 split and scraped vanilla bean
3/4 cup unsalted butter
3 cups whipping cream
1/4 cup rum

Combine egg yolks, egg, sugar, vanilla and salt in a large bowl. Whisk in milk and cream; strain through a fine strainer.

Preheat oven to 325 degrees. Arrange croissant pieces in an 11x7x2-inch baking pan. Pour as much custard as needed to soak croissants, leaving a little of the croissants visible on top; cover with foil. Put pan into a larger pan; fill with enough hot water to come half way up the sides of the smaller pan. Bake 45 minutes, or until knife inserted in center comes out clean. Remove from water bath and cool to room temperature to serve. Serve with Mulled Sultanas and Rum Vanilla Bean Caramel Sauce. Serves 8 to 10.

Mulled Sultanas

Put cranberries, raisins, sugar, rum, cinnamon, cloves, nutmeg and enough water to cover ingredients into a large saucepan. Simmer 20 minutes. Serve at room temperature. Makes about 2 cups.

Rum Vanilla Bean Caramel Sauce

Put water into a heavy medium saucepan and add sugar; but do not stir. Add vanilla bean: do not stir. Cook over medium heat until dark in color; swirl pan if necessary but do not stir. Watch carefully; do not let burn. Stir in butter over low heat; add cream, then rum. Serve warm. Cover and refrigerate extra sauce for future use. Makes about 5 1/2 cups.

🍎 Enjoy in moderation. Plenty for 16 servings.

🍇 Rosenblum Black Muscat; Rutherglen Show Muscat (Australia).

FACING PAGE FROM LEFT: *Tim Keating, DeVille; Louis Cressy, Bistro Lancaster.*

FOLLOWING PAGE: *Carl Walker, Brennan's.*

BEEF DEBRIS GUMBO
CORNMEAL DROP BISCUITS
ROOT VEGETABLE SLAW *with Ginger Vinaigrette*
OATMEAL CUSTARD
CHOCOLATE MOLTEN SOUFFLÉ *with White Chocolate Sauce*

Brennan's offers Houston a taste of Creole tradition. It comes from Alex Brennan-Martin's New Orleans restaurant family dynasty of Commander's Palace, Mr. B's, Palace Café, Bacco and Redfish Grill. The Commander's Palace kitchen was like Brennan-Martin's home.

Some legendary Brennan specialties will always be on the menu — Turtle Soup, Eggs Hussard, Bread Pudding Soufflé. But Brennan-Martin and award-winning executive chef Carl Walker are collaborating on bringing new culinary excitement to Brennan's, now in its 31st year here.

Homey favorites take on new sophistication. Crawfish is transformed in Crawfish Enchiladas or Nantua Crawfish Bisque under a pastry dome or made into a Creole étouffée broth and paired with locally raised redfish; the finishing touch is a pecan rice cake. Mahi Mahi is dressed up with Pontchartrain Sauce. Few can resist the decadent desserts from classic Bananas Foster and White Chocolate Bread Pudding to Chocolate Molten Soufflé. Walker's penchant for oatmeal as a child led to one popular dessert, Oatmeal Custard.

Walker grew up in rural Missouri, where his family was almost self-sufficient. They smoked and cured meats, kept the root cellar stocked with vegetables and canned goods and churned butter (his grandmother's CB radio "handle" was Country Butter). After his mother went back to work in town, Carl took care of his little sister after school, did his regular chores and also prepared dinner for the family, poring over cookbooks and magazines for inspiration.

At 17, he joined the Marines and went to cooking and baking school. Later he graduated from the Culinary Institute of America in Hyde Park, N.Y. In the '80s, several jobs in Houston led him to New Orleans, where he ended up at Commander's Palace. Then Houston beckoned again, and he became the chef at Brennan's.

The kitchen was expanded last year and a dining area and several private rooms were added. The focus is on quality and simplicity and developing a distinctive Texas-Creole cuisine to carry into the next 30 years, Walker says. That means developing the best sources for produce such as Creole tomatoes, field greens and mushrooms.

Brennan-Martin and Walker both grew up hunting and fishing and they are always alert to tracking down the best venison, ostrich, chukar, pheasant and quail.

LITE FARE

Creole classics include roux, gumbo and remoulade—all typically high in fat and sodium. It is best to choose from the Seasonal Specials, which often include a Seasonal Vegetable Platter. This kitchen is flexible and able to prepare food the way you want it. Special requests are honored.

Brennan's
3300 Smith St.
Houston, Tx 77006
713-522-9711

BEEF DEBRIS GUMBO

2 tablespoons oil or meat drippings
1 1/2 cups (cut in 1/2-inch dice) onion
1/2 cup (cut in 1/2-inch dice) red bell pepper
1/2 cup (cut in 1/2-inch dice) green bell pepper
1 cup cut okra (optional)
2 tablespoons minced garlic
6 cups beef broth, divided
3 bay leaves
1 tablespoon Louisiana hot sauce
1 tablespoon Worcestershire sauce
2 teaspoons Creole seasoning, such as Tony Chachere
1/4 teaspoon dried thyme leaves
4 cups (cut in 1/2-inch dice) cooked beef round roast (about 2 pounds)
3 to 4 tablespoons Creole Brown Roux (recipe follows)
4 cups assorted greens (kale, turnip, spinach, mustard, collards, Swiss chard and parsley), torn into 1-inch pieces
  Salt and freshly ground black pepper to taste
1/2 pound crawfish boudin, or your favorite, cut 1/4-inch thick
  Cornmeal Drop Biscuits (recipe follows)
2 teaspoons filé powder

CREOLE BROWN ROUX

2 cups vegetable oil
3 cups all-purpose flour
1/3 cup chopped yellow onion
1/3 cup chopped green bell pepper
1/3 cup chopped celery
1 teaspoon minced garlic

Heat oil to the smoking point in a large, heavy stockpot. Sauté onion, red and green peppers until onion is translucent. Add okra; sauté 1 minute. Add garlic and 1 cup broth to deglaze bottom of pan, when it starts to get dry. Add bay leaves, hot sauce, Worcestershire, Creole seasoning, thyme, beef and remaining 5 cups broth.

Bring to a simmer over medium heat and add Creole Brown Roux. This will give the gumbo flavor and body. It should be thick enough to coat back of a spoon. Simmer 15 to 20 minutes. Add greens; simmer until greens are wilted. Remove bay leaves; adjust seasoning with salt and pepper.

To serve, garnish top of gumbo with boudin and accompany with Cornmeal Drop Biscuits. Sprinkle filé over gumbo just prior to serving. Serves 8.

Creole Brown Roux

Heat oil almost to smoking point in a heavy 4-to-6-quart saucepan. Whisk flour in 1/4 cup increments into oil, cooking until flour gets a dark nutty brown before adding next portion. Stir constantly so flour doesn't burn on bottom of pan. When all flour is incorporated, remove from heat and add onion, pepper, celery and garlic. This will cool the roux, bringing out more color and adding flavor. Transfer roux to another pan; cool and refrigerate; reserve for later use. Some of the oil will rise to top; mix it in when ready to use.

🍎 Reduce oil to 1 tablespoon for sautéing. Use low-sodium broth. Reduce beef to 2 cups (about 1 pound). Eliminate added salt and boudin.

🍇 Beringer White Zinfandel or Fall Creek Chenin Blanc; Chateau Montcontour Vouvray (France).

CORNMEAL DROP BISCUITS

1	cup all-purpose flour
1/4	cup yellow cornmeal
1 1/2	teaspoons baking powder
1/4	teaspoon soda
1/2	teaspoon salt
3	tablespoons unsalted butter
1/2	cup milk
1/4	cup buttermilk
1/4	cup shredded jalapeño Jack cheese

Preheat oven to 375 degrees. Measure flour, cornmeal, baking powder, soda and salt into mixing bowl. Cut in butter with pastry blender (or two knives) until very fine. Make a well and pour milk and buttermilk in all at once. Add cheese; mix with a fork just until incorporated.

Drop eight portions with a spoon onto a greased baking sheet. Bake 15 minutes, or until nicely browned. Makes 8 biscuits.

 Biscuits are a higher-fat bread. Use moderation.

ROOT VEGETABLE SLAW *with Ginger Vinaigrette*

3/4	cup julienned celery root
3/4	cup julienned fennel
3/4	cup julienned carrots
2	tablespoons minced parsley
1/2	cup tat soi* leaves (spicy Japanese green resembling watercress)
1/2	cup mizuna* (delicate Japanese salad green)
1/2	cup Ginger Vinaigrette (recipe follows)

Separately blanch (drop into boiling water 1 minute): celery root, fennel and carrots until just tender; plunge into ice water. Drain until dry on absorbent towel, about 15 minutes. Combine blanched vegetables, parsley, tat soi and mizuna in bowl and toss with Ginger Vinaigrette to coat. Serves 4 to 6.

*See Special Helps section.

GINGER VINAIGRETTE

1/2	cup vegetable oil
1/4	cup rice wine vinegar
1/4	cup (cut in 1/4-inch dice) Red Delicious apple
1/2	teaspoon minced fresh mint
1	tablespoon peeled, minced ginger root
	Salt and freshly ground black pepper to taste

Ginger Vinaigrette

In small bowl whisk oil, vinegar, apple, mint and ginger root. Season with salt and pepper. Refrigerate unused portion for future use. Makes about 1 cup.

 Use 1/4 cup of Vinaigrette for slaw.

Enjoy without wine.

OATMEAL CUSTARD

5	eggs, beaten
1 1/2	cups milk
3/4	cup whipping cream
1	cup plus 2 tablespoons brown sugar
1	teaspoon ground cinnamon
2 1/2	cups cooked oatmeal, cooled
1/2	teaspoon vanilla extract
1	cup mixed fresh raspberries and blackberries, plus extra for garnish
	Whipped cream for garnish

Preheat oven to 350 degrees. Mix eggs, milk and cream; strain to fully incorporate egg into mixture; discard any residue. Combine egg mixture with sugar, cinnamon, oatmeal, vanilla and berries; stir lightly until mixed. Butter or spray with nonstick cooking spray 8 (1-cup) ramekins.

Fill ramekins with custard to within 1/4 inch of top; set in a baking pan and fill with water to within 3/4 inch of top of ramekins. Cover pan with foil; bake about 1 hour. Remove from water bath. Serve warm, garnished with a dollop of whipped cream, raspberries and blackberries. Serves 8.

 To lower cholesterol, use egg substitute for whole eggs.

Chateau Pena Muscat de Rivesaultes (France); Paul Jaboulet Muscat de Beaumes de Venise (France).

CHOCOLATE MOLTEN SOUFFLÉ *with White Chocolate Sauce*

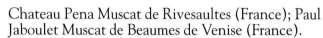

5	eggs
1	cup sugar
10	ounces semi-sweet chocolate, melted
6	tablespoons butter, melted
1	cup all-purpose flour
	White Chocolate Sauce (recipe follows)
	Powdered sugar for garnish

Preheat oven to 325 degrees. Cream eggs and sugar in a medium bowl; carefully scrape sides of bowl. Add chocolate and butter; blend well. Stir in flour; blend well.

Generously grease 6 (1-cup) soufflé cups with butter. Pour batter into cups and bake 15 to 20 minutes. May be prepared up to this point and stored in refrigerator several hours until ready to bake. If chilled, add a little baking time.

Meanwhile, prepare White Chocolate Sauce. Pour pool of sauce on each of 6 plates. Immediately unmold soufflés onto sauce. Dust tops with powdered sugar. Serves 6.

WHITE CHOCOLATE SAUCE

3/4	cup whipping cream
4	ounces white chocolate, such as Callebaut, melted

White Chocolate Sauce

Heat cream in small saucepan until almost boiling. Whisk cream into chocolate until smooth. Refrigerate until ready to use. Makes a generous 1 cup.

Enjoy in moderation. Serve 12 smaller portions.

Hermitage Road Shiraz (Australia); D'Arenberg "Custodian" Grenache (Australia); Jordan "J" Sparkling Wine.

STUFFED MUSHROOM APPETIZER *with White Wine Butter Sauce & Corn Relish*
GREEN ENCHILADAS (ENCHILADAS VERDES)
THREE MILK CAKE (PASTEL DE TRES LECHES)
CEVICHE *with Avocado Cream Sauce*

It might seem a stretch that an unassuming native Houstonian with Louisiana roots would be influenced by the Tarascan Indians from the Michoacan mountains deep in Mexico.

But Alan Mallett, already an experienced chef with a degree in dietetics and nutrition, got a call one day from his former boss, Bill Sadler. He asked Alan to be the chef of his new Mexican restaurant, Café Noche. Inconveniently, Alan knew next to nothing about Mexican cooking.

"I had to cram an awful lot of research into a short amount of time," he said. He became fascinated. By the time the restaurant opened in 1991, he was a pro.

"The cuisine of the Mexican interior is filled with rich flavors — chilies and fresh herbs and spices, especially cinnamon and fresh oregano." With his creative bent, he was soon improvising on the authentic dishes, making them fresher and more contemporary.

Today Café Noche is basically a Mexican herb kitchen, where everything is cooked from scratch. There are a few acknowledgements of Alan's Louisiana background. Imagine Blackened Chicken accompanied by two sauces — a creamy avocado and fire-roasted red pepper — or intriguing cabrito empanadas baked in puff pastry.

"I believe in basic, straightforward, hearty and earthy food," said Alan. That's why his Tortilla Soup is authentic: its spicy, rich chicken broth originated with the Tarascan Indians. Chilies en Nogado, a Mexican classic served at special holidays, is a poblano pepper filled with a spicy beef, pork and chicken mixture, battered, fried and topped with walnut sauce studded with fresh pomegranate seeds.

The vegetarian fare also gets tops marks — from Spinach Enchiladas and Quesadillas to a Vegetarian Tamale Plate.

The food is presented in the inviting background of a stucco hacienda with arched windows, carved stone columns and hand-carved wooden doors. A patio with lush flowers, plants and a fountain is a favorite meeting place for downtowners or Montrose residents. Changing displays of paintings and other artwork expose diners to some of Houston's favorite artists.

Guests often congregate at the bar, especially when the Saturday brunch or Sunday buffet attracts capacity crowds. Brunch includes omelets and other egg dishes as well as waffles, Mexican pastries and fresh fruit. A scaled-down lunch menu is designed for those on a short time schedule.

LITE FARE

Healthy Mexican food is hard to find but this restaurant offers some low-fat alternatives. Steamed vegetables can be substituted for rice and beans and baked chips for fried. You will find no lard, only vegetable oils on this menu. Dishes are made to order so special requests are honored.

Café Noche
2409 Montrose Blvd.
Houston, Tx 77006
713- 529-2409

STUFFED MUSHROOM APPETIZER
with *White Wine Butter Sauce & Corn Relish*

- 1 cup White Wine Butter Sauce (recipe follows)
- 1 cup Corn Relish (recipe follows)
- 1 (6-ounce) whole portobello mushroom
- 1/8 pound crabmeat, cleaned and picked over
- 1 cup shredded Monterey Jack cheese

Prepare White Wine Butter Sauce and Corn Relish. Preheat oven to 400 degrees. Grill mushroom 5 minutes on charcoal or barbecue grill; place in aluminum plate. Cover with crabmeat and top with cheese. Bake 8 minutes. Cut into triangles and arrange on serving plate; garnish with White Wine Butter Sauce and Corn Relish. Serves 3.

WHITE WINE BUTTER SAUCE

- 2 tablespoons chopped shallots
- 1 cup butter at room temperature, divided
- 1 bay leaf, crumbled
- 4 to 5 whole black peppercorns
- 1 cup dry white wine
- 1 cup white vinegar
- 1 cup whipping cream
- 1/4 teaspoon salt
- 1/4 teaspoon white pepper

White Wine Butter Sauce

Sauté shallots in 1 teaspoon butter in medium skillet until clear. Do not let brown. Add bay leaf, peppercorns, wine and vinegar; cook over medium heat until all moisture is evaporated. Add cream and cook until reduced by half. Remove from heat and swirl in remaining butter, 1 tablespoon at a time. Strain; add salt and pepper. Hold at room temperature (will keep 2 to 3 hours). Cover and refrigerate extra for future use. Makes 1 1/2 cups.

CORN RELISH

- 2 cups corn kernels cut from the cob or whole kernel canned corn
- 2 tablespoons finely diced onion
- 2 tablespoons finely diced red bell pepper
- 2 tablespoons finely diced green bell pepper
- 1/4 teaspoon salt
- 1/4 teaspoon white pepper
- 1 tablespoon white vinegar
- 2 tablespoons olive oil

Corn Relish

Mix corn, onion and bell peppers in medium glass or ceramic bowl; sprinkle with salt and pepper. Add vinegar; toss with oil. Cover and refrigerate until ready to serve. Makes 2 1/3 cups.

- Eliminate White Wine Butter Sauce and use 2 teaspoons oil in Corn Relish. Reduce cheese to 1/4 cup.

- Lindeman's Chardonnay Bin 65 (Australia); Kendall Jackson Chardonnay Grand Reserve.

GREEN ENCHILADAS (ENCHILADAS VERDES)

Tomatillo Sauce (recipe follows)
1 (2 1/2-pound) whole chicken
2 quarts water
1/2 onion, sliced
2 garlic cloves
Salt to taste
9 (6-inch) corn tortillas
Oil for frying tortillas
3/4 cup shredded Monterey Jack cheese
3/4 cup shredded Cheddar cheese

TOMATILLO SAUCE

25 tomatillos (Mexican green tomatoes), husked*
3 quarts water
1 onion, chopped
2 tablespoons garlic powder
2 tablespoons fresh chopped jalapeños
3 avocados peeled and sliced

Prepare Tomatillo Sauce. Put chicken into large stockpot with water, onion, garlic and salt; bring to a boil, reduce heat and simmer about 30 to 40 minutes, or until meat almost falls from bones. Remove chicken from water; discard skin. Pull meat from bones and shred; reserve.

Preheat oven to 450 degrees. Warm tortillas in a little hot oil in skillet just until pliable. Fill with shredded chicken and roll up. Arrange in shallow 2-quart rectangular pan; pour Tomatillo Sauce over enchiladas, top with combined cheeses. Bake 5 minutes, or until cheese melts. Serve with rice and refried black beans. Serves 3 (3 enchiladas each).

Tomatillo Sauce

*Dump tomatillos into sink of hot water to make husking easier. Bring 3 quarts of water to a boil; add tomatillos, onion, garlic powder and jalapeños. Reduce heat to medium and simmer 30 minutes; discard water. Blend in food processor with avocado until smooth.

Use just 1 avocado in Tomatillo Sauce. Eliminate oil to soften tortillas and warm them in the microwave by wrapping 6 tortillas in a damp paper towel and microwave on high 45 seconds. Serve 1 enchilada.

Domaine Pierredon Côtes du Rhone (France); Truchard Syrah.

THREE MILK CAKE (PASTEL DE TRES LECHES)

3/4 cup plus 2 tablespoons butter
1 3/4 cups sugar
8 egg yolks
1 cup milk
2 1/2 cups all-purpose flour
2 1/2 teaspoons baking powder
1/2 teaspoon salt
2 teaspoons vanilla extract, divided
6 eggs, separated
2 cups evaporated milk
1 (14-ounce) can sweetened condensed milk
3 1/2 cups half-and-half
1 (3-ounce) package cream cheese
1 1/2 tablespoons cream or milk
3/4 cup powdered sugar
Whipped cream, fresh berries and mint sprigs for garnish (optional)

Preheat oven to 350 degrees. Grease and flour a 12x8x2-inch pan; set aside. Cream butter and sugar in medium bowl. Add 8 egg yolks and 1 cup milk. Slowly mix in flour, baking powder, salt and 1 teaspoon vanilla; mix until batter is thick.

In separate bowl, beat 6 egg whites until stiff; fold into batter and pour into prepared pan. Bake 40 minutes, or until edges are golden brown. Remove from oven and cool in pan on rack. Poke holes in cake with a fork.

Blend evaporated milk, condensed milk and half-and-half with 6 egg yolks in blender or food processor. Bring half of this mixture to a boil in a saucepan, stirring constantly. Remove from heat and stir in remaining mixture. Brush over cake.

Blend cream cheese and cream in medium bowl until soft and fluffy. Beat in sugar gradually. Add remaining 1 teaspoon vanilla; beat until creamy. Spread evenly over cooled cake. Cut into wedges and garnish with whipped cream, fresh berries and mint sprigs. Store cake covered in refrigerator. Serves 8.

Enjoy this cake but in smaller portions – 16 servings.

Quady Electra Orange Muscat 1/2 bottle; Peter Lehmann Sauternes 1/2 bottle (Australia).

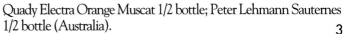

CEVICHE *with Avocado Cream Sauce*

Ceviche is one of the most popular dishes in the states of Guerro and Acapulco.

1/4 pound snapper fillets
1/4 pound salmon fillets
1/4 pound shrimp, peeled and deveined
1/4 pound scallops
2 cups fresh lime juice
1/2 teaspoon salt
1/4 white onion, diced
1 tomato, diced
1/2 fresh jalapeño, diced
1/4 cup chopped cilantro leaves
1/4 cup ketchup
1 tablespoon olive oil
1/4 teaspoon Worcestershire sauce
1/4 teaspoon Mexican hot sauce (Cholula recommended)
1/4 teaspoon dried oregano
Avocado Cream Sauce (recipe follows)
Tortilla strips and cilantro leaves for garnish
4 slices avocado, cubed

AVOCADO CREAM SAUCE

1 tablespoon diced onion
1 teaspoon clarified butter
1 tablespoon white wine
1/4 cup whipping cream
1/2 cup mashed avocado
1 teaspoon fresh lemon juice
Salt and freshly ground black pepper to taste

Cut snapper and salmon into 1x1 1/2-inch pieces. Cut shrimp and scallops into bite-size pieces. Combine snapper, salmon, shrimp and scallops in a glass bowl; cover with lime juice and salt. Cover and refrigerate 24 hours.

Drain seafood and place in clean bowl. With plastic spatula, stir in onion, tomato, jalapeño, cilantro, ketchup, oil, Worcestershire, Cholula sauce and oregano. Cover and refrigerate 1 hour. Prepare Avocado Cream Sauce.

Serve in cocktail glasses garnished with Avocado Cream Sauce, tortilla strips, cilantro leaves and cubed avocado. Serve with crackers. Serves 4.

Avocado Cream Sauce

Sauté onion and butter until clear. Add wine and reduce by half over medium heat. Add cream; reduce until thick. Combine cream mixture, avocado and lemon juice in food processor; blend until smooth. Season with salt and pepper. Can be served warm or chilled.

Ceviche is a low-fat recipe without the Avocado Cream Sauce. To include the sauce, eliminate salt and oil in Ceviche and reduce the Avocado Cream Sauce to 1 tablespoon per serving.

Trefethen Riesling; Schoffit Riesling (France).

FACING PAGE FROM LEFT: *Alan Mallett, Cresencio Salgado, Cafe Noché; Tommy Leman, Napoleon Palacios, Damian's.*

FOLLOWING PAGE FROM LEFT: *Hessni Malla, La Tour d'Argent; Greg Torres, Cavatore; Arturo Boada, Solero.*

FRIED CALAMARI (FRITTI DI CALAMARI)
MUSSEL SOUP (ZUPPA DI COZZE)
SHRIMP GIULIANA (SCAMPI GIULIANA)
CHICKEN GROGORIO (POLLO ALLA GROGORIO)
VEAL MARSALA   FETTUCCINE ROMA

More than 100 years ago, it was a real country barn in Bastrop, Texas. Now the barn is one of the most atmospheric restaurants in the city. About 15 years ago, owners of the popular French restaurant, La Tour d'Argent in northwest Houston, were looking for a concept for an Italian restaurant they wanted to build across the street. A friend suggested they use a barn since La Tour was built from an old log cabin.

They found the perfect barn in Bastrop, and co-owner Sonny Lahham had it disassembled, numbered the boards and transported them to Houston. A frame was built so the building could be insulated and the barn was reassembled around it. Lahham found enough metal panels for the roof by advertising in the newspaper for rusty metal.

One advantage of a barn is its size, which makes it a perfect background for a profusion of decorative objects. Co-owner Giancarlo Cavatore, an avid collector of memorabilia, has created an almost museum-like interior. Guests are treated to a fascinating display of old movie posters (including originals of Fellini's "8-1/2"), banners from Italy's 1984 world soccer championship, vintage photographs, flags, old advertisements, strings of garlic and family mementos. The Cavatore coat of arms comes from a small medieval village in northern Italy and is more than 800 years old.

For many loyal customers, Cavatore is the restaurant of choice for celebrating life's special occasions. It's a favorite for office gatherings, corporate entertaining, afternoon meetings, birthday parties, lunch with friends, wedding rehearsal dinners and retirement parties. A pianist plays nightly.

Many specialties have achieved star status on the menu — Fettuccine Alfredo, fried calamari, Veal Francese, Veal Milanese and Eggplant Parmigiana. Chef Greg Torres also offers several low-fat, low-cholesterol specials. Recent additions to the menu include Salmon with Aioli Sauce, Pork Tenderloin with Green Pepper Sauce and, at lunch, grilled T-bone steak with garlic and herbs.

A tempting assortment of desserts, all made in-house, is presented on the dessert tray. Chocolate mousse served in a chocolate shell (there's also a white chocolate version) and Turtle Cheesecake are top contenders.

The always-popular bar is a station for conversation, and guests have their pick of an in-depth list of wines including Italian classics such as Barolos and Chianti Riservas.

LITE FARE

Check out the Chef's Special Low-Calorie section for dishes prepared with a minimum of oil but an abundance of taste. Pastas come in appetizer and regular sizes; choose the appetizer portion for a lighter meal. Pastas are also divided into "fresh" which usually contain eggs and oil and "dry" which are relatively fat-free.

Cavatore
2120 Ella Blvd.
Houston, Tx 77008
713-869-6622

FRIED CALAMARI (FRITTI DI CALAMARI)

1	pound squid, cleaned and sliced into rings
	All-purpose flour
1/2	cup olive oil
1/2	cup unsalted butter
16	(21/25 count) shrimp, peeled and deveined
2	green onions, chopped
	Juice of 2 lemons
1/3	cup white wine
	Salt and freshly ground black pepper to taste
2/3	cup fish stock
6	ounces white crabmeat, cleaned and picked over

Dip squid in flour; remove excess. Heat oil in nonstick skillet; sauté squid until golden brown. Remove squid; set aside. Drain oil, melt butter in same skillet and sauté shrimp 4 minutes. Add onion and sauté lightly. Add lemon juice, wine, salt and pepper; cook 2 minutes. Add stock, squid and crabmeat; simmer 2 minutes. Serve on platter garnished with fresh basil leaves if desired. Serves 4.

Reduce squid to 1/2 pound. Reduce oil to 2 tablespoons and eliminate butter.

Trefethen Eschol White; Chablis Joseph Drouhin (France).

MUSSEL SOUP (ZUPPA DI COZZE)

4	(4-ounce) fish fillets, such as snapper
	All-purpose flour
1/2	cup olive oil, divided
16	mussels in shell
5	garlic cloves, sliced
1	cup dry white wine
16	sea scallops
12	(21/25 count) shrimp, peeled and deveined
1 1/2	(8-ounce) cans tomato sauce
2	tablespoons chopped fresh basil
	Salt and freshly ground black pepper to taste

Preheat oven to 225 degrees. Dust fish lightly with flour. Heat half the oil in heavy skillet; sauté fish in hot skillet 3 minutes each side. Transfer fish to ovenproof platter and place in oven while preparing rest of recipe.

Sauté mussels in same hot skillet until they open, adding more oil if necessary. Add garlic and wine; reduce 2 minutes. Add scallops and shrimp; sauté 5 minutes, adding more oil if necessary. Add tomato sauce and basil; simmer 5 minutes. Season with salt and pepper.

To serve, remove fish from oven, divide among 4 plates and top each fillet with seafood mixture. Serves 4.

Limit oil to 1/4 cup and substitute a low-sodium tomato sauce for regular. Serve with fat-free accompaniments such as plain rice and steamed vegetables.

Anselme Soave San Vincenzo (Italy); Regaleali Nozze d'Oro (Italy).

SHRIMP GIULIANA (SCAMPI GIULIANA)

1/2   cup unsalted butter, divided
20   (12/15 count) shrimp, peeled
      and deveined
      All-purpose flour
5   garlic cloves, sliced
1   teaspoon crushed red pepper
      flakes
      Salt and freshly ground black
      pepper to taste
2   tablespoons fresh chopped basil
4   tablespoons finely chopped
      parsley, divided
1/2   cup white wine
1/4   cup fresh lemon juice

Melt 6 tablespoons butter in a medium skillet. Lightly dip shrimp in flour; sauté in hot skillet 3 minutes each side, or until shrimp turn pink. Add garlic, red pepper, salt, black pepper, basil and 2 tablespoons parsley; cook 2 minutes.

Pour in wine. Flambé, lighting carefully with a taper match; add lemon juice, remaining 2 tablespoons butter and 2 tablespoons parsley. Reduce over medium heat until thickened. Serves 4.

🍎 Cut butter to 1/4 cup and serve with 1 cup plain rice.

🍇 Brotte Viognier (France); Pio Cesare Cortese de Gavi (Italy).

CHICKEN GROGORIO (POLLO ALLA GROGORIO)

4   boneless, skinless chicken
      breast halves (about 1 1/2
      pounds total)
      All-purpose flour
      Salt and freshly ground black
      pepper to taste
1/2   cup unsalted butter
1/2   pound mushrooms, sliced
1/2   large green bell pepper, seeded
      and sliced
1/2   large red bell pepper, seeded and
      sliced
1/2   cup dry white wine
3/4   cup whipping cream
3/4   cup shredded Cheddar cheese
3/4   cup shredded mozzarella cheese

Dust chicken with flour seasoned with salt and pepper. Melt butter in a medium skillet over medium-high heat; sauté chicken 4 minutes each side. Add mushrooms and green and red peppers. Sauté about 3 minutes (being careful not to overcook); peppers should remain crunchy.

Pour in wine. Flambé, lighting carefully with a taper match. Add cream and bring to a boil. Reduce heat and add cheeses; stir. Serve with pasta and a chunky tomato sauce. Serves 4.

🍎 Reduce butter to 1/4 cup. Substitute half-and-half for cream and reduce to 1/2 cup. Substitute low-fat Cheddar for regular and part skim mozzarella for regular; reduce each to 1/4 cup. Serve with low-fat pasta and tomato sauce.

🍇 Firesteed Pinot Noir; BV Pinot Noir Carneros or Erath Pinot Noir (Oregon).

VEAL MARSALA

1	pound veal scaloppine
	All-purpose flour
	Salt and freshly ground black pepper to taste
1/2	cup unsalted butter, divided
1/2	pound white mushrooms, sliced
2	tablespoons chopped green onion
1/2	cup Marsala wine
3/4	cup brown sauce (see Special Helps section)

Dust veal slices with flour seasoned with salt and pepper. Melt 1/4 cup butter in a hot skillet; lightly sauté veal 1 minute on each side. Add mushrooms, onion and more butter, if needed. Cook 3 minutes; pour in wine. Flambé, lighting carefully with a taper match. Stir in brown sauce and remaining 1/4 cup butter. Reduce until thickened, about 3 minutes. Serve with Fettuccine Alfredo and spinach sautéed with garlic and Parmesan. Serves 4.

🍎 Reduce butter and brown sauce to 1/4 cup each. Serve with a low-fat pasta.

🍇 Ricasoli Chianti Classico (Italy); Brolio Chianti Classico Riserva (Italy).

FETTUCCINE ROMA

1	pound fresh or dry fettuccine
1/2	cup unsalted butter, divided
16	(16/20 count) shrimp, peeled and deveined
1/2	pound white mushrooms, sliced
4	tablespoons chopped green onions
1/2	pound lump crabmeat, cleaned and picked over
1	cup whipping cream
	Salt and freshly ground black pepper to taste
3/4	cup freshly grated Romano cheese
	Fresh basil leaves and chopped parsley for garnish (optional)

Cook pasta in large stockpot of boiling water until al dente. Drain; set aside and keep warm. Melt 1/4 cup butter in a medium skillet; sauté shrimp 4 minutes. Add mushrooms and onion; sauté 3 minutes. Toss crabmeat with shrimp mixture.

Combine pasta, cream and remaining 1/4 cup butter in large saucepan. Season with salt and pepper. To serve, divide pasta and sauce among 4 plates, top with shrimp and crabmeat mixture; garnish with Romano, basil and parsley. Serves 4.

🍎 Limit butter to 1/4 cup by eliminating butter added to pasta. Substitute half-and-half for cream. Use 1/4 cup cheese.

🍇 Bollini Pinot Grigio (Italy); Ruffino Cabrea (Italy).

WHITE GAZPACHO
ROASTED FLOUNDER WITH GARLIC & BACON
WALNUT TART *with Jack Daniel's Ice Cream*
VEGETABLE RAGOUT WITH CHERVIL

After tasting the food at Chez Nous, it's hard to believe that many of the exceptional dishes evolved from the meager diet that owner Gerard Brach remembers from his childhood. Born in Alsace in Strasbourg, one of the gastronomic centers of Europe, he was sent to live with his grandparents when his parents divorced and his father moved to Africa.

His grandfather was a fisherman and could never predict what he would be able to catch and sell. His grandmother was an expert at stretching bits of this and that into a meal. Bread Soup was almost a daily certainty because French bread was always on hand. His grandmother would add a few vegetables from the garden and occasionally a bit of fish, and the resulting soup was brought to the table again daily until all was eaten.

A growing boy, Brach figured that he would be less apt to go hungry if he helped his grandmother in the kitchen; that's where he learned to cook. He left home at 14, went to Austria where he worked in a small hotel, then to North Africa where he lived with his father and learned Arabic. He also worked in Alsace, Germany and on the French Riviera before coming to the United States in 1961.

All these culinary experiences have influenced his cooking; his menus are strong in the classics — veal, escargots, scallops, fresh foie gras, duck, quenelles. But for contrast there are innovative creations — duck mousse with plum wine and pickled cherries; a salad of crab, mango, avocado, tomato and basil; steamed salmon with lemongrass, pink pickled ginger, chilies and lemon risotto. Menus change daily but always include the signature rack of lamb. Brach sells about 5,000 a year. He only uses New Zealand lamb raised to his specifications. Fresh fish is delivered weekly from fish markets in England and Chile.

Chez Nous consistently receives top ratings as one of Houston's best restaurants. It has received the DiRoNA award for distinguished restaurants of North America and the Best of the Best Five Star Diamond Award from the National Academy of Restaurants and Hospitality Sciences.

Fifteen years ago Brach and his wife Sandra converted a small Pentecostal church into the French farm cottage-style restaurant where figs, avocados, peaches and tomatoes grow just outside the back door. Brach's daughter, Danielle Noble-Brach, is maitre d'. Two private rooms are available for small parties, weeknights only. Reservations are a must; make them as far ahead as possible for weekends.

LITE FARE

The French Paradox challenges the assumption that you can't eat high-fat meals and be healthy. Is it the red wine, olive oil or northern fish high in omega-3 fats that counter the high-fat sauces? Or could it be moderation and exercise? Enjoy this superb restaurant in moderation. Special requests are taken seriously.

Chez Nous
217 S. Ave. G
Humble, Tx 77338
281-446-6717

WHITE GAZPACHO

1 1/2 cups cubed white bread, crusts removed and soaked in water
3 cups ice water
3 cups seedless green grapes
2 1/2 cups sliced almonds
4 1/2 tablespoons white vinegar
1 tablespoon chopped garlic
1 cup extra-virgin olive oil
Salt and freshly ground black pepper to taste
Sliced almonds and grapes for garnish

Squeeze bread cubes to remove excess water. Place bread, ice water, grapes, almonds, vinegar and garlic in blender; puree. With blender running, slowly add oil in a thin stream. Season with salt and pepper. Serve ice cold garnished with almonds and grapes. Serves 12.

🍎 Eat in moderation.

🍇 Monte Volpe Moscato d'Mendocino; Lava Cap Muscat Canelli.

ROASTED FLOUNDER WITH GARLIC & BACON

1 (1 1/2-to-2-pound) whole flounder, cleaned
1/4 cup all-purpose flour, seasoned with salt and freshly ground black pepper to taste
1 tablespoon olive oil
1/4 pound applewood bacon, cut into 1-inch by 1/2-inch strips
6 garlic cloves, poached in boiling water 7 minutes
2 tablespoons finely chopped shallots
2 tablespoons sherry vinegar
1/4 cup chicken broth
1/4 cup whipping cream
1/4 cup cold unsalted butter, cut in small pieces
1 (10-ounce) package fresh spinach, washed

Preheat oven to 400 degrees. Lightly coat fish with seasoned flour. Heat oil in ovenproof skillet. Add fish and sauté over medium heat until golden on one side. Turn fish over, add bacon and garlic; sauté until fish is golden. Place skillet in oven and bake 8 minutes, or until fish is just cooked. Transfer to warm serving dish, spoon garlic and bacon over fish; cover with aluminum foil to keep warm.

Pour off excess fat from skillet. Add shallots; sauté until softened. Deglaze with vinegar; add broth and cream. Cook 2 minutes to reduce, or until thickened. Whisk in butter, a few pieces at a time. When sauce is smooth, pour over fish and serve with spinach, which has been blanched in salted water and lightly sautéed in butter. Serves 2.

🍎 Limit bacon to 1/8 pound (2 slices). Substitute half-and-half for cream and reduce butter to 2 tablespoons.

🍇 R.H. Phillips Toasted Head Chardonnay; Franciscan Chardonnay or Robert Mondavi Chardonnay; Kumeu River Chardonnary (New Zealand) or Puligny-Montrachet Joseph Drouhin (France).

WALNUT TART *with Jack Daniel's Ice Cream*

TART SHELL

5	tablespoons butter
1/4	cup sugar
3	tablespoons solid all-vegetable shortening
1	egg
1 1/2	cups all-purpose flour
1 1/2	teaspoons baking soda
1	teaspoon salt

FILLING

1	cup unsalted butter
1/2	cup honey
1/4	cup granulated sugar
1	cup packed brown sugar
3 1/4	cups chopped walnuts
1/4	cup whipping cream
	Jack Daniel's Ice Cream (recipe follows)
	Your favorite chocolate and/or caramel sauces for garnish
	Berries and mint sprigs for garnish

JACK DANIEL'S ICE CREAM

6	eggs or equivalent egg substitute (see Note)
2 1/4	cups sugar
4	cups milk
3	cups whipping cream
3/4	cup Jack Daniel's whiskey

Combine butter, sugar, shortening and egg in electric mixer with paddle beater and beat until smooth. Mix flour, soda and salt and combine with butter mixture until it forms a smooth ball. Roll out into a 10-inch pie shell and fit into pie or tart pan with removable bottom. Trim edges by rolling a rolling pin across top of pan.

Filling

Combine butter, honey, white and brown sugars in a nonreactive saucepan (such as ceramic or stainless steel). Stir until combined, then bring to a simmer and cook 5 minutes, or until bubbling. Add walnuts and cream; blend thoroughly. Let cool 15 minutes. Prepare Jack Daniel's Ice Cream.

Preheat oven to 350 degrees. Pour filling into tart shell and bake 35 minutes, or until firm (center should barely wobble). Remove from oven, cool 30 minutes and refrigerate until ready to serve.

To serve, cut tart into wedges. Stripe dessert plates with sauces in a decorative pattern; place tart over sauces. Top with Jack Daniel's Ice Cream and a mint sprig. Garnish with berries. Serves 12.

Jack Daniel's Ice Cream

Combine eggs, sugar, milk, cream and Jack Daniel's; blend thoroughly and freeze in ice cream maker according to manufacturer's directions. Makes about 2 quarts.

Note: If concerned about using raw eggs because of the risk of salmonella poisoning, use egg substitute or your favorite recipe for a cooked custard ice cream.

 Enjoy in moderation.

 Gentleman Jack Bourbon 375 ml (Tennessee); Chateau de Laubade Bas Armagnac (France).

VEGETABLE RAGOUT WITH CHERVIL

8	baby carrots
3	small white turnips, peeled
2	small zucchini
10	small white onions, peeled
6	tablespoons unsalted butter, divided
1	cup sliced green cabbage
1	cup broccoli florets
1/2	red bell pepper, diced
1/2	teaspoon olive oil
1/2	cup cold water
1	teaspoon lemon juice
	Salt and freshly ground white pepper to taste
1/4	cup chopped chervil leaves

Slice carrots, turnips and zucchini into similar sized pieces. Place carrots, turnips, zucchini and onions in 4 separate small saucepans, adding just enough water to cover. Add 1 tablespoon butter to each pan and cook over medium heat 3 to 7 minutes; drain and use juices in vegetable soup.

Blanch cabbage and broccoli separately in boiling water to cover 2 minutes. In small skillet, sauté bell pepper in oil over medium heat 2 minutes.

In large heavy saucepan, melt remaining 2 tablespoons butter; add carrots, turnips, zucchini, onion, cabbage, broccoli and bell pepper. Deglaze with water and lemon juice. Season with salt and pepper. Serve in a deep dish; garnish with chervil. Serves 6 as a main course and 12 as an appetizer.

This recipe is a good source of vitamins A and C. To reduce fat, eliminate butter added to vegetables while boiling in water and use just 1 tablespoon for sautéing. Eliminate oil.

Tyrell's Long Flat Red (Australia); Côte de Beaune-Village Faiveley or Aloxe-Corton Domaine Senard (France).

FACING PAGE FROM LEFT: *Gerard Brach, Danielle Noble-Brach, Stephan Gasaway, Chez Nous.*

FOLLOWING PAGE FROM LEFT: *Allan Levine, Clive Berkman, Clive's.*

Oven Baked Salmon on Rock Salt
Creamed Spinach
Sirloin and Ribeye Rub   Steak Cooking Tips
Dijon Vinaigrette
Sticky Toffee Cake *with Caramel Sauce*

Clive's is moving to a new beat. The renamed, renovated Charley's 517 in the downtown theater district represents several trends — the revitalization of downtown Houston, renewed interest in fine beef and steak houses and the popularity of more casual restaurants that offer good values in food, wine and live entertainment.

Clive Berkman, who was managing director of Charley's, is the creative force behind the restaurant's new upbeat personality and streamlined menus. Signature dishes include Pecan Grilled Buffalo Tenderloin and Oven Roasted Rack of Texas Lamb along with down-home lunch specials such as smothered pork chops and chicken fried tenderloin.

CLIVE'S

Berkman, a native of Johannesburg, South Africa, has been interested in good food since he was a child (at age 6 he devoured a jar of caviar from the refrigerator as a snack). His mother, now an author, cooking teacher and caterer in New York, has been a major influence. As a child, he watched her conduct cooking classes in their home in South Africa.

Experiences as an officer's mess cook in the South African infantry convinced him to become a professional. He studied cooking and hotel and restaurant management in England where he earned a master's degree. Berkman also worked and studied in vineyards and wineries in France and Germany. He helped set up a wine program at the Hilton College of Hotel and Restaurant Management at the University of Houston. Clive's award-winning wine cellar provides selections to complement any dish and includes more than 90 ports and cognacs. The cellar turns into a lively jazz bar on weekends.

Lunch attracts the business crowd, but with the energized downtown scene, many return in the evening. Loyal customers still come for the signature crab cakes, hearts of palm salad, lump crabmeat and classic Caesar, but pecan-grilled steaks, chicken and salmon have made new friends.

They like the idea of selecting a favorite cut of meat prepared to order — char-grilled, pecan-grilled, pan-seared or oven-roasted. Berkman and executive chef Allan Levine developed distinctive dry spice rubs, sauces and condiments to give each dish special personality.

As a consultant, Berkman has revamped several restaurants in Galveston for entrepreneur George Mitchell including The Wentletrap, which was renamed Charley's 517 at the Wentletrap. Other ventures include Créme de la Créme catering company and True Concessions, which provides food at theaters and outdoor festivals.

--- *Lite Fare* ---

Clive's offers personal attention and honors all food requests. Preparation options include char-grilled, pecan-grilled, pan-seared and oven-roasted. All these can be done with little or no added fat. As an accompaniment choose the Sweet Pepper Relish. A Seasonal Vegetable Platter is on both the lunch and dinner menus.

*Clive's
517 Louisiana
Houston, Tx 77002
713-224-4438*

OVEN BAKED SALMON ON ROCK SALT

Rock salt
2 (8-ounce) salmon fillets, scaled with skin on

Preheat oven to 450 degrees. Scatter salt in thin layer in a baking pan. Place fillets 1-inch apart on top of salt, skin side down. Bake 10 to 12 minutes, until just cooked, or to desired doneness. Remove salmon from salt; carefully scrape away extra salt crystals, skin and dark salmon meat from bottom side. Can be served hot, warm or at room temperature with choice of accompaniments. Serves 2.

 Limit portion size to 6 ounces.

Argyle Pinot Noir (Oregon); Kent Rasmussen Pinot Noir.

CREAMED SPINACH

2 (10-ounce) packages frozen chopped spinach
4 garlic cloves, minced
1 small onion, finely diced
1/4 cup unsalted butter
2 tablespoons all-purpose flour
1 cup whipping cream
1 tablespoon sugar
 Zest of 1 lemon
 Pinch of nutmeg
 Salt and freshly ground black pepper to taste
 Freshly grated Parmesan cheese for garnish

Thaw spinach; chop in blender or pulse in food processor until spinach is almost pureed; reserve.

Sauté garlic and onion in butter in small saucepan until onion is translucent. Whisk in flour; continue to cook until light golden color. Whisk in cream; add sugar and zest. Bring mixture to a simmer and cook 10 minutes. Season with nutmeg, salt and pepper.

To finish; heat spinach in medium skillet. Add sauce and bring to a rolling simmer. Heat thoroughly. Place in serving dish; garnish with Parmesan. Serves 6 to 8.

 Reduce butter to 2 tablespoons. Substitute evaporated skim milk for cream.

SIRLOIN AND RIBEYE RUB

3/4	cup white peppercorns
3	tablespoons black peppercorns
2	bay leaves
1	tablespoon whole coriander
2	tablespoons dried basil leaves
2	tablespoons dried thyme leaves
1	tablespoon dried tarragon leaves
1	teaspoon paprika
1/2	teaspoon garlic powder
1/2	teaspoon onion powder
1/2	teaspoon ground oregano
1/2	teaspoon brown sugar
1/4	teaspoon ground ginger
	Pinch of cayenne

In spice grinder or coffee mill, finely grind white peppercorns, black peppercorns, bay leaves and coriander. Combine with basil, thyme, tarragon, paprika, garlic and onion powders, oregano, sugar, ginger and cayenne. Season meat with mixture before cooking.

 Great low-sodium seasoning.

Parducci Petite Syrah; Quivira Zinfandel or De Loach Zinfandel; Sean Thackery Orion.

STEAK COOKING TIPS

1) Select the finest quality meats. For sirloins and ribeyes, the fat should be trimmed to 1/4-inch or less. Steak should be cut 1-inch in thickness at a minimum.

2) Meat should be allowed to sit at room temperature 30 minutes before cooking.

3) Liberally season meat with selected herb rub or seasonings and salt. For grilling, coat lightly with olive oil.

4) For pan seared steaks, heat skillet on medium-high heat. Sear meat in a small amount of clarified butter or desired oil (a blend of canola, extra-virgin olive oil and porcini oil adds a delicious flavor).

5) Steaks should be placed near the hottest part of the fire on the grill but not directly over the hot spot.

6) Cook meat slightly under desired finished doneness and allow meat to rest 5 to 10 minutes before serving. Steaks will still be hot and at the appropriate doneness.

7) Steaks will be most juicy and flavorful when cooked to medium rare.

DIJON VINAIGRETTE

1	shallot, quartered
1	garlic clove
1/3	cup rice wine vinegar
1	tablespoon Dijon mustard
1 1/2	teaspoons dried thyme leaves
	Salt and freshly ground black pepper to taste
1	cup extra-virgin olive oil

Put shallot, garlic, vinegar, mustard, thyme, salt and pepper in blender; puree. While motor is running, add oil in slow stream until dressing is emulsified. Cover and refrigerate. Makes 1 1/2 cups.

🍎 Enjoy in moderation — use 2 tablespoons per serving.

STICKY TOFFEE CAKE *with Caramel Sauce*

1 1/2	(8-ounce) packages chopped pitted dates
2	cups water
1/4	cup butter
1 1/2	cups sugar
4	eggs
1/2	teaspoon vanilla extract
2 1/2	cups cake flour (such as Swan's Down)
2	teaspoons baking soda
	Caramel Sauce (recipe follows)

Preheat oven to 375 degrees. Grease a 13x9x2-inch baking pan. Combine dates and water in saucepan and cook until reduced to a jam consistency, stirring often. Reserve.

Cream butter and sugar in electric mixer. Add eggs and vanilla. Add reserved date mixture. Combine flour and baking soda; add to mixture; mix thoroughly by hand.

Bake 20 to 25 minutes. Prepare Caramel Sauce. While hot, poke cake thoroughly with a skewer or toothpick. Pour Caramel Sauce over cake, reserving some for garnish. Serves 12.

CARAMEL SAUCE

1 3/4	cups packed brown sugar
1 1/2	cups coffee cream
1	cup butter
1	teaspoon vanilla extract

Caramel Sauce

Combine sugar, cream, butter and vanilla in saucepan; bring to a boil and boil 5 minutes. Use with cake. Makes about 4 cups.

🍎 To lower cholesterol, use 2 whole eggs and 4 egg whites. In Caramel Sauce, substitute half-and-half for cream. Use only half of sauce on cake.

🍇 KWV Noble Late Harvest Riesling 1/2 bottle (South Africa); Miles Malmsey Madeira (Portugal).

Thomas' Salad (Insalata Tomasso)
Stuffed Pork Loin (Lombo Porchetta Imbottire)
Dominic's Penne Pasta (Penne alla Dominic)
Marsala and Mascarpone Zabaglione with Strawberries

Damian's is one of the Bayou City's favorite destinations for business lunches and celebratory occasions from birthdays and anniversaries to wine tastings and wedding rehearsal dinners. An upstairs banquet room accommodates 120 and is a frequent setting for corporate entertaining. The chef's table looking out on the kitchen is a convivial setting for six-course prix fixe gourmet dinners with appropriate wines. The bar is a convenient place to meet for a drink or wait for a table.

The menu at Damian's is a little like a Mandola family history. Involtini di Pollo, Shrimp Damian, Snapper Nino Jr., Pollo alla Gratella, Gamberoni Vincenzo and other specialties are based on dishes that have been on Mandola family tables for generations. Some are embellished or updated after the owners and chefs travel to Italy periodically, but there's always a sense of family connection. Present owners, Frank B. Mandola and Joseph "Bubba" Butera, who bought the restaurant in 1993, are cousins of the original owner, Damian Mandola.

Executive chef Napoleon Palacios is assisted by sous chef, Tommy Leman, who moved to Italy and worked in restaurants there after he graduated from the Culinary Institute of America in Hyde Park, N.Y. They turn authentic, fresh ingredients into memorable meals. There are daily specials at lunch and dinner and a different hand-made ravioli daily. Fresh fish has become so popular that the restaurant often goes through 100 pounds at lunch.

If guests aren't in a hurry to leave, it's because the dessert menu is so tempting. Guests are compelled

to have a cappuccino or espresso with Lemon Tart or Chocolate Infusione, Damian's three-chocolate version of Death by Chocolate. Or they may order several desserts and share — great candidates for round-the-table tasting are Panna Cotta, an Italian molded cream, Sicilian Bread Pudding with Whiskey Hard Sauce and Coupelle, zabaglione whipped with mascarpone cheese and layered with fresh berries.

Those in the know may just order Italian cookies. Made from Mama Grace Mandola's recipes, they are baked on premise, retaining all the old-world character.

The dining room looks up to window boxes of flowers at the street level. Muted terra cotta walls, rustic antiques, framed family photographs, wooden tables with starched white linens and fresh flowers give the low-ceilinged arched dining room home-like warmth and charm.

──────── *Lite Fare* ────────

Italian restaurants have the basics of healthy eating—lean meats and seafood, good complex carbohydrates in pasta and bread and fresh vegetables. It's the sauces that add the fat. Marinara or clam sauce is usually lowest in fat. A frequent special request is grilled snapper with steamed or grilled vegetables.

Damian's
3011 Smith St.
Houston, Tx 77006
713-522-0439

THOMAS' SALAD (INSALATA TOMASSO)

1/2	cup Insalata Tomasso Dressing (recipe follows)
6	ounces romaine
6	ounces arugula
4	ounces endive
4	ounces radicchio
	Butter
12	(1/2-inch diagonally cut) slices baguette bread
10	ounces goat cheese (log form)
1/2	cup finely chopped mixed fresh herbs, such as basil, rosemary and thyme
10	ounces prosciutto di Parma, thinly sliced and grilled

Prepare Insalata Tomasso Dressing. Wash romaine, arugula, endive and radicchio; pat dry and chop. Combine lettuces in bowl (allowing 1 cup per person); set aside. Preheat oven to 300 degrees.

Lightly butter baguette slices and toast in oven 5 to 10 minutes, until lightly golden and crisp. Slice goat cheese into 12 equal portions; dredge both sides of cheese in chopped herb mixture. Place each piece of cheese on baguette slice; reserve.

Toss salad greens with dressing; divide among 6 plates. Warm prosciutto and cheese-topped baguette slices in oven 2 to 3 minutes. Alternate 2 baguette slices and 2 slices prosciutto around edge of greens. Serves 6.

INSALATA TOMASSO DRESSING

1/3	cup finely diced red bell pepper
1/3	cup finely diced red onion
2	garlic cloves, minced
2	tablespoons coarsely chopped fresh basil
1/4	cup red wine vinegar
2	tablespoons balsamic vinegar
3	tablespoons whole grain mustard
2	tablespoons freshly grated Parmesan cheese
3/4	cup extra-virgin olive oil
1/2	teaspoon salt
1	teaspoon freshly ground black pepper

Insalata Tomasso Dressing

Combine bell pepper, onion, garlic, basil, red wine vinegar, balsamic vinegar, mustard and Parmesan in a medium bowl. Slowly whisk in oil, drop by drop, until all oil is incorporated and a stable emulsion is formed. Or prepare in blender. Season with salt and pepper. Cover and refrigerate extra for future use. Makes about 2 cups.

🍎 Eliminate butter and prosciutto. Reduce cheese to 2 ounces and spread 1 teaspoon on each bread slice. Reduce dressing to 6 tablespoons.

🍇 Argiolas Perdera (Italy); Allegrini "La Grola" Valpolicella (Italy).

STUFFED PORK LOIN (LOMBO PORCHETTA IMBOTTIRE)

Marinade (recipe follows)
1 (3-to-4-pound) bone-in pork loin
Spinach Stuffing (recipe follows)
Salt and freshly ground black pepper to taste
Mushroom Topping (recipe follows)

MARINADE

1/2 cup balsamic vinegar (12-year-old aged preferred)
3 tablespoons chopped fresh rosemary
2 tablespoons minced garlic
Salt and freshly ground black pepper to taste
2 cups extra-virgin olive oil

SPINACH STUFFING

1/4 cup extra-virgin olive oil
1 cup finely chopped onion
1/2 cup minced shallots
3 tablespoons minced garlic
5 bunches fresh spinach, stemmed and well washed
2 pounds mild Italian sausage, chopped
2 eggs
1 cup freshly grated Parmesan cheese
Salt and freshly ground black pepper to taste

MUSHROOM TOPPING

1/2 cup clarified butter (see Special Helps)
1/4 cup chopped fresh thyme leaves
18 ounces shiitake and cremini mushrooms,* trimmed and quartered
Salt and freshly ground black pepper to taste

Prepare Marinade. Trim pork loin of any silver skin and excess fat. Place pork loin in shallow pan; pour marinade over top. Cover and refrigerate at least 12 hours.

Prepare Spinach Stuffing. Preheat oven to 400 degrees. Remove pork loin from marinade. With sharp knife (such as a filleting knife), pierce center of pork loin and insert knife lengthwise until it comes out of other end, creating a slit in center of loin to place stuffing. Fill cavity with stuffing. An iced tea spoon is a handy tool for this.

Place pork in shallow pan; sprinkle with salt and pepper. Roast 10 minutes, reduce heat to 325 degrees and roast 1 hour, or until medium well-done (160 degrees internal temperature). Allow to rest 5 to 10 minutes. Prepare Mushroom Topping.

Slice meat into 1-inch chops, like a rack; garnish with topping. Serve 1 to 2 pieces per person. Accompany with roasted potatoes and grilled asparagus. Serves 6.

Marinade

Combine vinegar, rosemary, garlic, salt and pepper in medium bowl; whisk in oil slowly.

Spinach Stuffing

Heat oil in large skillet; sauté onion and shallots until translucent. Add garlic and sauté briefly. Add spinach and continue to sauté. Add sausage and cook until fully browned. Allow mixture to cool. Add eggs and Parmesan; mix well. Season with salt and pepper.

Mushroom Topping

Heat butter in medium skillet; add thyme and mushrooms. Sauté until done. Season with salt and pepper.

*Other exotic mushrooms such as morels and oyster mushrooms may be substituted.

Choose a lean, trimmed center cut of pork loin and reduce size to 3 pounds. Spinach Stuffing: reduce oil to sauté spinach to 2 tablespoons, eliminate sausage and reduce Parmesan to 1/4 cup. Mushroom Topping: reduce butter to 2 tablespoons.

Taurino Salice Salentino (Italy); Villa Pillo Syrah (Italy); Tommasi Amarone (Italy).

59

DOMINIC'S PENNE PASTA (PENNE ALLA DOMINIC)

3	red bell peppers
3	tablespoons extra-virgin olive oil, divided
1	pound penne pasta
1/2	pound fresh spinach
1	tablespoon minced garlic
1	cup whipping cream or half-and-half
1	cup ricotta cheese
	Salt and freshly ground black pepper to taste
1 1/2	pounds boneless, skinless chicken breasts, grilled

Rub bell peppers with 1 tablespoon oil. Place on preheated grill or open gas flame and cook until fully charred on all sides, turning as needed. Place in stainless steel bowl and cover with plastic wrap; allow to cool. When cool, peel skins off and cut in half lengthwise. Remove seeds and white ribs. Cut into 1/4-inch julienne strips; reserve.

Boil pasta in large stockpot of salted water until al dente. Meanwhile heat remaining 2 tablespoons oil in large skillet; sauté spinach and garlic. Add roasted pepper and cream; cook over medium heat until thickened and reduced slightly.

When pasta is cooked, drain and add to sautéed mixture (reserving some of the pasta water). Fold in ricotta and sauté briefly. Adjust consistency with pasta water, if needed. Season with salt and pepper. Slice chicken into strips; arrange on top of pasta. Serves 6.

Eliminate 2 tablespoons oil by sautéing spinach and garlic in 1/4 cup low-sodium chicken broth. Substitute half-and-half for cream and skim milk ricotta for regular.

Sella & Mosca Cannonau di Sardegna (Italy); Coppo "Camp du Rouss" Barbera d'Asti (Italy).

MARSALA AND MASCARPONE ZABAGLIONE WITH STRAWBERRIES

6	egg yolks
1/2	cup packed brown sugar
1/4	cup dry Marsala wine
1	tablespoon brown sugar
1 1/2	teaspoons dry Marsala wine
1/2	cup mascarpone cheese, softened
2	tablespoons whipping cream
3	pints fresh strawberries, washed and hulled

For zabaglione, whisk yolks and 1/2 cup sugar in top of double boiler until smooth. Whisk in 1/4 cup Marsala. Place over simmering water and beat until slowly dissolving ribbon forms when whisk is lifted, about 5 minutes. Remove top of double boiler; place on counter and cool mixture to room temperature, whisking occasionally.

Dissolve 1 tablespoon sugar in 1 1/2 teaspoons Marsala in custard cup. Beat mascarpone with cream in another bowl until thickened. Add dissolved sugar and Marsala; beat until thick and light. Fold in yolk mixture.

Divide berries among 6 bowls. Top each with zabaglione and serve. Serves 6.

Note: If mascarpone cheese is unavailable, blend 6 ounces cream cheese with 3 tablespoons whipping cream and 2 tablespoons sour cream.

 Enjoy in moderation.

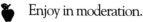 Buton Brandy (Italy).

GOUGÈRES
TEXAS GULF COAST LUMP CRAB CAKES *with Ginger Soy Butter*
ROASTED SWEET GARLIC WHIPPED POTATOES
TAHITIAN VANILLA FRUIT SOUP

Tim Keating's sophisticated menus don't hint that he began his career at 13 on the New Jersey shore as a potwasher. One of a family of 10, he was raised on simple food — bread topped with cheese and tomato soup poured over it was a frequent supper.

But just as he progressed from potwasher to cook to caterer to one of the highest profile chefs in the country, Keating's menus also have progressed. At DeVille, the fine dining restaurant at the Four Seasons, one of Houston's finest hotels, guests dine globally. In addition, Keating works with contacts in Seattle and Portland and along the Gulf Coast to buy fish from day boats. He has arrangements with four local organic farmers to provide the highest quality vegetables, herbs and edible flowers.

The chef, who moved to the West Coast when he was 18, broadened his restaurant experience and started his own catering company in San Diego. He also has worked as executive sous chef to world-class chef Jacques Maximin at the Meridien Hotel, traveled in France and served as chef at luxury hotels in California, New York and Houston. Keating gained major recognition for events such as the Dinner of the Decade held in Houston in 1995 to support and honor the James Beard Foundation and Houston's Society for the Performing Arts. He invited eight of the nation's award-winning chefs to join him in that event. A dinner Keating and six top chefs produced here to honor world-renown chef Paul Bocuse was the culinary event of the year in 1996.

At the Four Seasons Hotel, Keating continues the tradition of excellence that has earned DeVille, among other awards, the AAA Four Diamond Award for eight consecutive years and the DiRoNA Award for six consecutive years. Another coveted honor is the Zagat Restaurant Survey top awards from 1994 to 1997 for Best Service, Top Hotel Dining, Top New American Cuisine, Top Sunday Brunch and Top Rooms Décor. He supervises all food served in the hotel including weekend brunches, 24-hour room service and catering. Menus change frequently, sometimes daily.

FOUR SEASONS HOTEL
Houston

"I'm very religious about two things — using fresh food in season to support local farmers (we don't make blackberry cobbler in December) and giving the food an identity. We're focusing on a modern French-style of cuisine with Mediterranean flavors."

--- *LITE FARE* ---

Chef Timothy Keating believes in seasonally fresh ingredients and collaborates with local growers to provide the freshest, tastiest foods available, many organically farmed. Look for items designated as Alternative Cuisine—selections nutritionally balanced and lower in calories and fat. Vegetarian items are also marked. Vegetables and grains abound on this menu.

DeVille
Four Seasons Hotel
1300 Lamar
Houston, Tx 77010
713-650-1300

GOUGÈRES

A simple, delightful, easy-to-make, inexpensive snack that is served throughout the great winemaking regions of France.

1	cup water
5	tablespoons unsalted butter
1	teaspoon salt
1/4	teaspoon freshly ground black pepper
1/4	teaspoon freshly ground nutmeg
1	cup all-purpose flour
1	cup shredded Swiss or Gruyère cheese
5	eggs, divided
1/2	teaspoon water
1/2	cup freshly grated Parmesan cheese

Preheat oven to 425 degrees. Grease baking sheet; set aside. Bring water, butter, salt, pepper and nutmeg to a boil in a medium saucepan. Remove pan from heat. Stir in flour all at once and beat with a wooden spoon until mixture leaves the sides of pan. Add cheese; beat until well incorporated. Beat in 4 of the eggs, one at a time until thoroughly absorbed and mixture is smooth and shiny.

Drop mixture by small teaspoonfuls onto baking sheet. Beat remaining egg with water; brush tops of each pastry with egg wash. Sprinkle top of each with a bit of Parmesan and bake in upper third of oven 20 minutes, or until golden brown. Makes about 3 dozen bite-size pieces.

Enjoy in moderation.

Drink literally any table wine, white or red, with these little snacks.

TEXAS GULF COAST LUMP CRAB CAKES
with Ginger Soy Butter

1/2 pound jumbo lump crabmeat, cleaned and picked over
4 egg whites
1/2 red bell pepper, finely diced
1/2 jalapeño pepper, finely diced
1/4 cup fresh fine white bread crumbs
1 tablespoon fines herbes
 Kosher salt and freshly ground black pepper to taste
 Ginger Soy Butter (recipe follows)
6 tablespoons olive oil, divided
2 bunches fresh spinach, washed
4 large shiitake mushrooms, cleaned and sliced
4 large oyster mushrooms, cleaned and sliced
 Chicken broth, if needed
 Diced tomatoes and fresh herb sprigs for garnish

GINGER SOY BUTTER

1 1/2 teaspoons sesame oil
1 shallot, diced
1 teaspoon finely diced fresh lemon grass
1 teaspoon grated fresh ginger
1/4 cup white wine
1/2 cup chicken broth
2 tablespoons low-sodium soy sauce (Tamari recommended)
1/4 cup unsalted butter, cut into pieces

Gently toss crabmeat, egg whites, bell pepper, jalapeño, bread crumbs, fines herbes, salt and pepper until well blended. Roll mixture into a 2-inch diameter tube shape, wrap in plastic wrap and refrigerate 1 hour.

Make Ginger Soy Butter; reserve. Cut crabmeat tube into 4 patties. Heat 2 tablespoons oil in medium skillet, sear patties until lightly browned on each side; reserve.

Heat 2 tablespoons oil in same skillet; sear spinach until just wilted, about 30 seconds. Season with salt and pepper; divide and place in center of each plate. In same pan, heat remaining 2 tablespoons oil; add mushrooms; cook until tender. Add a little broth if pan gets too dry. To serve, place crab cake on top of spinach; top with mushrooms and garnish with Ginger Soy Butter, diced tomatoes and a fresh herb sprig. Serves 4.

Ginger Soy Butter

Heat oil in small saucepan; "sweat" shallots, lemon grass and ginger 2 minutes over low heat. Do not brown. Add wine; cook until reduced by three-fourths. Add broth and soy sauce; cook until reduced by one-fourth. Remove from heat and add butter, one piece at a time, whisking continuously. Strain through fine strainer and reserve in warm place. Makes about 1/2 cup.

🍎 Reduce oil to a total of 2 tablespoons by substituting chicken broth to wilt spinach and cook mushrooms. Limit Ginger Soy Butter to 1 tablespoon per serving.

🍇 Chateau Bonnet Blanc (France); Quivira Sauvignon-Blanc Reserve.

ROASTED SWEET GARLIC WHIPPED POTATOES

4   large baking potatoes (such as russets)
1   cup milk (or cream if desired), warmed, divided
    Sea salt and freshly ground black pepper to taste
3   whole large heads elephant garlic
2   tablespoons canola oil
4   tablespoons extra-virgin olive oil, divided

Preheat oven to 450 degrees. Peel and cut potatoes into large pieces. Cook in medium saucepan in salted water until tender when pierced with a fork, about 15 minutes. Drain potatoes well and place on a sheet pan. Dry out in oven 8 to 10 minutes, or until they turn white and are no longer moist to the touch. Put potatoes through a hand ricer or food mill then transfer to an electric mixer bowl or food processor. Whip well using paddle attachment (or steel blade for processor). Add 3/4 cup milk and season with salt and pepper; beat until well blended. Set aside and most importantly, keep warm.

Reduce oven temperature to 350 degrees. Roast garlic heads in canola oil 25 minutes. Peel and puree in a small food processor.

When ready to serve, heat a medium saucepan; add potato mixture and garlic puree. Immediately add remaining 1/4 cup milk and "work" with a wooden spoon 4 to 5 minutes, beating constantly. Add olive oil, 1 tablespoon at a time; beat until very smooth. Serve immediately. Serves 4.

Notes: Never refrigerate pureed potato mixture; always keep warm, serve with favorite roasted chicken or meat. Any leftover potato mixture may be refrigerated and used the next day for splendid potato pancakes.

 Use low-fat (2%) milk. Reduce canola oil to 1 tablespoon and olive oil to 2 tablespoons.

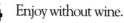 Enjoy without wine.

TAHITIAN VANILLA FRUIT SOUP

2   cups sugar
2   quarts water
    Zest of 5 oranges
    Zest of 5 lemons
3   vanilla beans
    Assorted seasonal fruits, such as: peeled oranges, melon, star fruit, papaya unpeeled pears and apples, whole grapes, or berries
    Fresh mint for garnish

Dissolve sugar in water in large saucepan over medium heat. Add orange and lemon zest. Split vanilla beans, scrape seeds from pod and add seeds and pods to mixture in saucepan. Bring to a boil; remove from heat and let steep 1 hour at room temperature. Cover and refrigerate mixture; remove vanilla pods and seeds. Makes 2 1/2 quarts.

To serve, prepare favorite fruits in season and toss with syrup mixture using 3/4 cup fruit and 1/2 cup syrup per person. Garnish with mint.

Note: Syrup may be stored in refrigerator as long as 1 month.

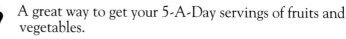 A great way to get your 5-A-Day servings of fruits and vegetables.

 Enjoy without wine.

FILET MIGNON A LA EMPRESS
STEAMED SALMON WITH FRESH GINGER AND SCALLIONS
CRISPY CHICKEN WITH GINGER, GREEN ONION SAUCE
LEMON BAKED CHEESECAKE

Guests at the award-winning Empress restaurant may not be aware that, along with sophisticated East-meets-West fusion cuisine, they are enjoying some of Mom's home cooking. Owner/chef Scott Chen has adapted several specialties from family recipes, and one of the most popular dishes is Filet Mignon a la Empress, Chen's mother's recipe. Her Taiwanese and Japanese influence is evident in many menu favorites.

Chen grew up in Taiwan where the family was involved in construction, the motor freight business and seafood production. He worked for his father for five years and spent two years in the military. Chen, a third degree black belt in judo, went to a sports school. When he decided to move to the United States in 1980, he took some basic cooking classes at the Taipei Hilton and concluded that he might like a career in food service.

After the family immigrated to the States, Chen traveled the country for five years working in restaurants of various ethnic cuisines. In Houston, he went to work for his sister-in-law, Wendy Wang, as a dishwasher at Ambassador Chinese Restaurant (see Page 17). He worked his way up at other Chinese restaurants and opened Empress in 1985.

EMPRESS

There he has developed his own style, progressing from Nouvelle Chinese to Pacific Rim to Fusion emphasizing fresh ingredients and healthful, low-cholesterol cooking. Chen has added his special touch to traditional Asian favorites on the menu. Another concept is White Glove Special Fusion Cuisine six-course dinners. Loyal customers are always intrigued by Chen's next creation and Houston fans are anxiously awaiting the opening of a restaurant inside the Loop.

Several prestigious restaurant awards — the DiRoNA, Best of the Best designation from the American Academy of Restaurant and Hospitality Sciences and several from the Wine Spectator — acknowledge his success. He has been a guest chef at the James Beard House in New York City several times and was included in a "Great Chefs, Great Cities" television series and accompanying cookbook.

Diners should be prepared for unexpected taste sensations at Empress — stuffed quail in a raisin Bordeaux sauce, grilled fresh foie gras in Bordeaux applesauce, stir-fried veal with fresh basil and fish with Japanese seasonings and miso sauce. Dishes are paired with compatible wines from a selection of 18,000 bottles representing more than 800 of the world's finest labels.

--- LITE FARE ---

East meets West on this menu of innovative and savory sauces combined with low-fat food preparation. Chef Scott Chen's special cooking techniques for low-fat preparation include "quick pre-boiling" and "flash sautéing." Enjoy the natural flavors of fresh foods. Vegetarian dishes are available and special requests are honored and encouraged.

Empress
5419-A FM 1960 West
Houston, Tx 77069
281-583-8021

FILET MIGNON A LA EMPRESS

1   (10-ounce) filet mignon
1   teaspoon soy sauce
1/2 teaspoon rice wine
1   teaspoon cornstarch
1   teaspoon freshly ground black pepper
1   tablespoon water
1   pound broccoli, divided into florets
1/2 cup olive oil, divided
1/2 teaspoon salt (optional)
2   teaspoons chopped green onion
2   teaspoons minced garlic
1/4 cup oyster sauce (Old Vintage recommended)
1   teaspoon sesame oil

Cut filet mignon into 1-inch squares. Toss meat with soy sauce, wine, cornstarch, pepper and water. Marinate at least 10 minutes at room temperature.

Divide broccoli florets into sections (save stems for another use). Cook broccoli 2 minutes in boiling water. Drain and plunge into cold water 2 minutes; drain thoroughly.

Heat skillet and add 2 tablespoons oil; heat until very hot. Add broccoli and salt; stir-fry about 1 minute; remove. Arrange florets around edge of platter. Heat same pan until very hot. Add 5 tablespoons oil and sauté meat cubes over medium heat until brown; remove.

Heat same skillet and add remaining 1 tablespoon oil. Add onion, garlic and oyster sauce; stir-fry until fragrant. Add meat cubes; stir-fry lightly, then add sesame oil. Toss again and remove to serving platter. Serves 2.

Use low-sodium soy sauce. Limit oil to 1 tablespoon to stir-fry beef. Use a cooking spray to stir-fry broccoli, onion and garlic. Eliminate added salt. Serve with plain rice.

Montes Alpha Merlot (Chile); Hogue Merlot (Washington); Vieux Chateau Certan (France) or Chateau Trotanoy (France).

STEAMED SALMON WITH FRESH GINGER AND SCALLIONS

1	tablespoon rice wine
2	teaspoons salt
2	pounds boneless salmon fillets
1/4	cup shredded green onions, tops only
1/4	cup shredded ginger
1	tablespoon balsamic vinegar (Old Vintage recommended)
2	teaspoons soy sauce
1	tablespoon sesame oil

Rub wine and salt over salmon; marinate at least 10 minutes. Place salmon on a rack in steamer; cover and steam 15 minutes over high heat. When salmon is cooked, remove and sprinkle onions, ginger, vinegar and soy sauce over fish.

Heat oil until smoking and pour over onions and ginger. The hot oil will bring out the flavor of the onions and ginger. Serve immediately. Serves 4.

🍎 Salmon is a higher fat fish but loaded with omega 3 fatty acids that can help lower your cholesterol. This is a low-fat preparation. Reduce sodium by using low-sodium soy sauce and eliminating added salt.

🍇 QC Fly Pinot Noir; Champy Beaune-Bressandes (France) or any of the Jadot Beaune wines (France).

CRISPY CHICKEN WITH GINGER, GREEN ONION SAUCE

4	(6-ounce) boneless, skinless chicken breast halves
1/2	teaspoon rice wine
3	teaspoons salt, divided
1/4	teaspoon freshly ground black pepper
1/3	cup cornstarch
3	cups oil for frying
4	teaspoons olive oil
1	cup minced green onion, tops only
3	tablespoons minced ginger
1/2	cup chicken broth

Rinse chicken breasts and pat dry. Place in medium bowl with wine, 1 teaspoon salt and pepper. Marinate 20 minutes. Remove and dredge chicken in cornstarch.

Heat wok or deep-fat fryer; add frying oil. Heat to 375 degrees. Deep-fry chicken until breasts are golden. Remove and drain on paper towels. Arrange on serving platter.

To prepare sauce: Heat olive oil in a small saucepan until very hot. Add onion, ginger, remaining 2 teaspoons salt and broth. Stir-fry until fragrant; pour over chicken. Serves 4.

🍎 Fry chicken quickly and drain well. To reduce sodium, eliminate added salt and use low-sodium chicken broth.

🍇 Latoure St. Chinian (France); Rectoria Collioure (France).

LEMON BAKED CHEESECAKE

Lemon-lovers will enjoy this non-traditional cheesecake.

1 1/3   cups all-purpose flour, divided
1/2   teaspoon salt
1/3   cup unsalted butter
4   tablespoons water, divided
1 1/2   (8-ounce) packages cream cheese, softened
2   eggs
3   tablespoons unsalted butter, melted
1/2   cup sugar
1/2   cup fresh lemon juice
1   teaspoon lemon zest
1/2   cup whipping cream (chill cream, beaters and bowl well)
Fresh blueberries or strawberries and mint sprigs (optional)

Preheat oven to 350 degrees. Combine 1 cup flour and salt in a medium bowl. Cut in 1/3 cup butter until pieces are size of small peas. Add 3 tablespoons water; toss with a fork until all flour is moistened and mixture begins to form a ball. Add more water to crumbs in bottom of bowl, if necessary. Gather dough into a flat ball. Roll out to a 12-inch circle. Fit pastry into a 10-inch springform pan, pressing to side and bottom. Do not stretch. Prick side and bottom with a fork; set aside.

Beat cream cheese, eggs and 3 tablespoons butter, sugar and lemon juice in large bowl. Sift remaining 1/3 cup flour gradually into cheese mixture; blend well. Add zest.

Whip cream in a separate bowl; fold carefully into cheese mixture. Pour into pastry-lined pan; smooth top. Bake until golden brown, about 1 hour and 30 minutes. Garnish with fresh blueberries, strawberries and fresh mint sprigs as desired. Serves 6.

 Enjoy in moderation.

Sandeman Ruby Port (Portugal); Fonseca Bin 27 Port (Portugal); De Fussigny Cognac (France).

FACING PAGE, FROM LEFT: *Scott Chen, Empress*

FOLLOWING PAGE, FROM LEFT: *John Sheely, Riviera Grill; Frederic Perrier, Grille 5115*

GOAT CHEESE SALAD WITH APPLE *and Sun-Dried Tomato Vinaigrette*
SALMON RISOTTO *with Red Pepper Cream Sauce*
SUSAN'S MOTHER'S CARROT CAKE *with Cream Cheese Frosting*

Frederic Perrier brings New York and French elan to Grille 5115 by Ruggles. It is a sophisticated cousin to Bruce and Susan Molzan's award-winning Ruggles in the Montrose area. When Perrier talks about home cooking he refers to Lyon in Burgundy, one of the world's most famous gastronomic regions.

Perrier began cooking at 13 and took a pre-apprenticeship in a school-work program. He quickly rose in the ranks after a two-year apprenticeship at La Mere Blanc. He worked in the French West Indies and at several two- and three-star restaurants in France before immigrating to the United States in 1985. Famous chef-cookbook author Pierre Franey became his mentor. Perrier later worked at La Cite, a busy Parisian-style brasserie and one of the best oyster bars in New York.

His next job, at a 70-seat French bistro in Greenwich Village, gave Perrier a different perspective. Among customers were the French ambassador and his wife, who later asked him to become chef at their residence on Park Avenue.

His marriage to native Houstonian Michelle Minton brought him here. The advent of the splendid Saks Fifth Avenue in the Galleria in September, 1997, offered the perfect opportunity. The restaurant has an art deco ambiance with interplay of reflections from glass, lighting, mirrors and burnished metals. Marble floors, polished woods and a swagged curtain of thousands of copper beads that covers one wall add to the grand setting. This dining room calls for dramatic food.

The Molzans, co-owners, contributed favorites from Ruggles — crabcakes, grilled vegetable plates, fresh fish dishes and lush desserts. Perrier, chef/co-owner added eclectic pizzazz.

The lunch menu dabbles in Mexican, Asian and other ethnic flavors, such as Baked Beans and Duck Quesadillas or Shrimp Dumplings with Lemon Grass Coconut Broth.

Grille 5115 is a destination restaurant for fine dining in the evening. After the store is closed, valet parking and an elevator make it easily accessible from the plaza level on the Westheimer side. It is a polished setting in which to savor such signature dishes as Pan-Seared Fresh Foie Gras with baked apples or Sweet Potato Risotto with Cabernet-Braised Short Ribs and Rock Shrimp. Choose the perfect wine from Grille 5115's extensive list.

Desserts include Chocolate Créme Brûlée Cheesecake, Coconut Cream Pie, Lemon Meringue Pie, White Chocolate Mousse and Tiramisu.

LITE FARE

An abundance of healthy items reside on the Grille 5115 menu. Enjoy a Roasted Vegetable with Fresh Herb Pizza that has no animal products—not even cheese; Fettuccini with Grilled Vegetables and Wild Mushrooms in a Roasted Garlic Broth (made with chicken broth); or try a special plate of Seasonal Vegetables prepared either steamed or grilled.

Grille 5115
Saks Fifth Avenue
5115 Westheimer
Houston, Tx 77056
713-963-8067

GOAT CHEESE SALAD WITH APPLE
and Sun-Dried Tomato Vinaigrette

1	head Bibb lettuce
1	head arugula
1	head red-leaf lettuce
8	ounces goat cheese, divided into 4 (2-ounce) patties
1/4	Granny Smith apple, julienned
4	sun-dried tomatoes, julienned
1/4	cup toasted almond slivers
	Salt and freshly ground black pepper to taste
1	cup Sun-Dried Tomato Vinaigrette (recipe follows)

Wash and dry greens; combine in large bowl. Divide mixed greens among 4 plates. Arrange cheese on top. Place apple on one side of cheese and sun-dried tomatoes on the other. Add almonds; sprinkle salt and pepper on top. Drizzle Sun-Dried Tomato Vinaigrette over salads. Serves 4.

SUN-DRIED TOMATO VINAIGRETTE

1/4	pound sun-dried tomatoes, julienned
1	tablespoon chicken seasoned stock base (see Special Helps section)
1	tablespoon Dijon mustard
1 1/2	teaspoons chopped garlic
1/2	cup fresh basil leaves
1/2	cup honey
	Salt and freshly ground black pepper to taste
2	cups olive oil

Sun-Dried Tomato Vinaigrette

Combine tomatoes, chicken base, Dijon, garlic, basil, honey, salt and pepper in blender; slowly add stream of oil through cap. Makes about 2 1/2 cups. Refrigerate extra.

Limit goat cheese to 4 ounces. Cut almonds to 2 tablespoons. Use just 2 tablespoons per serving of Sun-Dried Tomato Vinaigrette.

Jadot or Duboeuf Beaujolais-Villages (France); Pradeaux Bandol Rosé (France).

SALMON RISOTTO
with Red Pepper Cream Sauce

8   very ripe plum tomatoes
    Salt and freshly ground black
    pepper to taste
    Red Pepper Cream Sauce
    (recipe follows)
2   tablespoons butter, divided
2   tablespoons chopped shallots
1   tablespoon chopped garlic
1   cup Arborio rice
1/2 cup dry white wine
2   cups chicken broth
1/2 cup whipping cream
2   tablespoons chopped fresh basil
2   tablespoons chopped fresh
    cilantro leaves
2   tablespoons chopped fresh
    chives
1   tablespoon freshly grated
    Parmesan cheese
4   (8-ounce) salmon steaks
1   medium leek, julienned and
    fried

To oven-dry tomatoes: Heat oven to 350 degrees. Cut tomatoes into halves, season with salt and pepper, place on pan and oven-dry 2 hours; reserve.

Prepare Red Pepper Cream Sauce; reserve and keep warm. Melt 1 tablespoon butter in medium skillet; sauté shallots and garlic until transparent. Add rice; sauté 3 minutes, stirring. Add wine; let cook until wine is reduced and mixture is almost dry. Add broth; cook over low heat about 40 minutes, stirring almost constantly. When rice is al dente (firm to the tooth), add cream, remaining 1 tablespoon butter, basil, cilantro, chives and Parmesan.

Salt and pepper salmon. Grill over high heat to medium rare, about 6 minutes.

Divide risotto among 4 plates; place in center of each. Place salmon on top. Garnish plate with 4 tomato halves and balance a sheaf of julienned leeks on top of salmon. Spoon sauce between tomatoes. Serves 4.

RED PEPPER CREAM SAUCE

1   tablespoon olive oil
1   red bell pepper, seeded and
    diced
1   teaspoon chopped shallot
1   teaspoon chopped garlic
    Splash of white wine
1   cup whipping cream
    Salt and freshly ground black
    pepper to taste

Red Pepper Cream Sauce

Heat oil in small skillet; sauté bell pepper, shallot and garlic. Add wine; stir to deglaze pan. When almost dry, stir in cream. Simmer 15 minutes over low heat. Season with salt and pepper. Pour into blender; puree on high until smooth.

 Reduce butter to 1 tablespoon to sauté rice and use low-sodium chicken broth. Substitute half-and-half for cream. Use just 1/2 cup of the Red Pepper Cream Sauce.

Indigo Hills Pinot Noir; Wild Horse Pinot Noir

SUSAN'S MOTHER'S CARROT CAKE
with Cream Cheese Frosting

1 cup butter, softened
2 cups sugar
4 eggs
1 teaspoon vanilla extract
2 cups all-purpose flour
2 teaspoons baking soda
1 teaspoon salt
1 teaspoon ground cinnamon
3 cups grated carrots
Cream Cheese Frosting (recipe follows)

Preheat oven to 350 degrees. Grease and flour 2 (9-inch) layer cake pans; set aside. All ingredients should be room temperature. Cream butter until light. Add sugar; mix well. Blend in eggs one at a time; add vanilla.

Sift flour, soda, salt and cinnamon together. Add to butter mixture; beat until combined. Do not overmix. Stir in carrots.

Pour into prepared pans. Bake 30 to 40 minutes, or until cake springs back when lightly touched. Cool 20 minutes in pan on a cake rack. Turn cakes out and cool completely before frosting with Cream Cheese Frosting. Serves 8 to 10.

CREAM CHEESE FROSTING

1 1/2 (8-ounce) packages cream cheese, softened
1/2 cup unsalted butter, softened
2 teaspoons vanilla extract
6 cups powdered sugar, sifted
3/4 cup toasted pecan pieces

Cream Cheese Frosting

Beat cream cheese, butter and vanilla until smooth. Add sugar, 1 cup at a time; mix well. Fold in pecans. Spread between layers and frost sides and top of cake.

Good source of vitamin A. Enjoy in moderation. Serves 12 adequately.

Chateau Stony Muscat de Frontignan 1/2 bottle (France); Chateau St. Helen Sauternes 1/2 bottle (France).

SOUTHWEST CAESAR SALAD
JALAPEÑO BARBEQUED SHRIMP *with Pico de Gallo Rice*
MACADAMIA NUT CHOCOLATE CARAMEL TORTE

THE HOUSTONIAN

W hen Jim Mills was growing up in Beaumont, he planned to become a lawyer. Fortunately for lovers of fine dining in Texas, he became a chef. His considerable talent for turning simple foods into memorable creations brings him acclaim at the four-star, four-diamond ranked Houstonian Hotel, Club & Spa.

"Food is so much a part of place," says Mills. Take rice, for example. It is ubiquitous on Gulf Coast menus in Cajun-Creole dishes. But Mills gives it a different twist — the breakfast menu features risotto with dried apricots and nonfat cream cheese, a far cry from the rice-with-milk Mills occasionally ate for breakfast as a child.

The chef has been interested in cooking since he was a child. He used to help his mother in the kitchen and at 10 was making Cherries Jubilee for a dinner party dessert.

Mills interrupted his college career at the University of Texas to travel in Europe where he and a friend cooked their way across the continent with a camp stove and mess kit. He returned to UT, and determined to become a restaurant chef, he taught himself French cooking from cookbooks while performing as sole kitchen employee at a small café.

He left Austin again to become sous chef to J. Seward Johnson (of the Johnson & Johnson health products dynasty) in New Jersey. A few years later his career began to take off when he joined the Mansion on Turtle Creek in Dallas, where chef Dean Fearing was making a name for Southwestern cuisine. Mills was later hired as executive chef of the posh Hotel Crescent Court in Dallas.

There's a little bit of Beaumont and a lot of global panache in Mills' "Texas Harmonic" style. The Houstonian caters to health and fitness-minded guests who demand fresh, healthful foods. But they also want flavor and eye appeal. Calories and fat grams are listed for selected menu items.

The Houstonian is a peaceful get-away with restful views of towering pines, wooded walks and manicured flower beds and lawns. Many people are surprised to learn the restaurants are open to the public. Mills supervises food for the casually elegant restaurant, The Café, which is open to the public; 30 event and party rooms; The Center Court; room service; banquets; and the signature restaurant, The Manor House. It is located in a house designed by noted Houston architect, John Staub.

LITE FARE

For a really healthy dining experience, try the Houstonian's Healthy Dining Program that lists fat grams and calorie levels for all designated items. Fat is limited to 20% of calories but taste is not sacrificed. A full nutrient analysis is available for most recipes. The staff is knowledgeable and open to any special requests.

The Houstonian
111 N. Post Oak Lane
Houston, Tx 77024
713-680-2626

SOUTHWEST CAESAR SALAD

Spicy Caesar Dressing (recipe follows)
2 heads romaine lettuce
3/4 cup cooked black beans
3/4 cup roasted corn kernels
1/2 cup pumpkin seeds (pepitas) from a Mexican squash
1/2 cup cotija cheese (Mexican white cheese) or other queso fresco
Julienned multicolored tortilla chips, baked or fried, for garnish

Prepare Spicy Caesar Dressing. Wash, spin or pat lettuce dry. Tear into 1 1/2-by-1/2-inch pieces and place in large salad bowl. Add dressing and toss lightly. Add beans and corn; toss again. Divide mixture among 4 chilled plates. Sprinkle with pumpkin seeds and cheese. Garnish with tortilla chips. Serves 4 as an entrée salad.

SPICY CAESAR DRESSING

1 egg yolk
1 tablespoon minced garlic
2 teaspoons Dijon mustard
2 anchovy fillets, minced
1 1/2 teaspoons coarsely ground black pepper
1/4 teaspoon salt
1/2 teaspoon ground coriander
1/2 teaspoon ground cumin
1 teaspoon Worcestershire sauce
2 teaspoons cold water
1/2 cup extra-virgin olive oil
1/2 cup canola oil
1 1/2 tablespoons sambal chili paste (Thai chili paste)
Juice of 1/2 lemon
Juice of 1/2 lime
3 tablespoons freshly grated Parmesan Cheese

Spicy Caesar Dressing

Combine yolk, garlic, Dijon, anchovies, pepper, salt, coriander, cumin, Worcestershire and water in food processor; process until smooth. With motor running, pour oils in a slow, steady stream into egg mixture. When all oil has been incorporated, add chili paste, lemon and lime juices and Parmesan; process until smooth. Makes about 1 1/2 cups.

Note: The Houstonian uses pasteurized egg yolks. If concerned about using raw egg yolk because of the risk of salmonella poisoning, use egg substitute.

Good source of fiber (8 grams per serving). Reduce pumpkin seeds, cheese and dressing to 1 tablespoon of each per serving.

Franz Reh Piesporter Goldtröpfchen Kabinett (Germany); Van Kesselstatt Kaseler Nies'chen Kabinett (Germany).

JALAPEÑO BARBEQUED SHRIMP
with Pico de Gallo Rice

3   jalapeños, stemmed and seeded
4   garlic cloves, minced
1/2   cup coarsely chopped cilantro sprigs
     Juice of 1 1/2 limes
1   teaspoon cracked black pepper
1 1/2 teaspoons salt
24   (16/20-count) shrimp, peeled and deveined, tails left intact
     Pico de Gallo Rice (recipe follows)
1   tablespoon olive oil
1   tablespoon butter
     Cilantro sprigs and lime wedges for garnish

Place jalapeños, garlic, cilantro, lime juice, pepper and salt in food processor; pulse until mixture is evenly ground but chunky. Transfer to a small glass bowl and add shrimp. Stir well to coat shrimp with marinade, cover and refrigerate at least 2 but not more than 6 hours.

Prepare Pico de Gallo Rice; reserve. To cook shrimp, heat oil in large heavy skillet until almost smoking. Remove shrimp from marinade but do not wipe off mixture. Carefully add shrimp to skillet and sauté until the marinade just begins to turn golden. Add butter, reduce heat and cook until shrimp are done, stirring often.

To serve, place 3/4 cup rice on each plate and surround with 6 shrimp. Spoon some of marinade over shrimp. Garnish with cilantro and lime wedges. Serves 4.

PICO DE GALLO RICE

2   teaspoons canola oil
1/4   yellow onion, minced
1 1/2 cups Texas long-grain rice
2   cups chicken broth or water
1/2   bay leaf
1 1/2 teaspoons salt
2   tomatoes, seeded and diced
1/4   yellow onion, diced
1 1/2 jalapeños, stemmed and seeded, chopped
1/3   cup coarsely chopped cilantro sprigs
     Juice of 1/2 lime

Pico de Gallo Rice

Heat oil in medium saucepan; add minced onion and rice. Cook, stirring often, until rice is golden, then add broth, bay leaf and salt. Bring to a boil, cover and reduce heat; simmer 15 minutes. Add tomato, diced onion and jalapeños; re-cover and cook 5 minutes. Gently stir in cilantro and lime juice. Discard bay leaf; correct seasoning. Keep warm until served. Makes 5 1/2 cups.

Great low-fat recipe. To reduce sodium, eliminate added salt and use low-sodium chicken broth in Pico de Gallo Rice.

Domaine de Aubuisieres Vouvray Demi-Sec (France); Chateau Moncontour Vouvray Demi-Sec (France).

MACADAMIA NUT CHOCOLATE CARAMEL TORTE

Sweet pastry dough or pie crust to fit a 12-inch torte pan

10 ounces whole macadamia nuts, roasted until golden and cooled

8 ounces bittersweet chocolate, broken into medium chunks

1 cup granulated sugar

1 cup light corn syrup

1/2 cup plus 2 tablespoons unsalted butter, melted, divided

4 large eggs, lightly beaten

1/4 teaspoon ground cinnamon

Pinch of salt

1 cup packed brown sugar

1/4 cup water

Preheat oven to 300 degrees. Line a 12-inch torte pan with dough; crimp edge as desired. Combine nuts and chocolate chunks in medium bowl; pour into prepared torte shell. Mix sugar, corn syrup, 6 tablespoons butter, eggs, cinnamon and salt in medium bowl; pour over nuts and chocolate. Bake 35 minutes; remove from oven and drizzle with caramel syrup (directions below). Return to oven and bake 15 minutes.

While torte is baking, combine remaining 1/4 cup butter, brown sugar and water in a small saucepan. Cover and bring to a rapid boil. Cook 3 minutes, uncover and cook until caramel syrup is at softball stage (234 degrees on a candy thermometer). Keep warm until needed.

Cool torte until firm enough to remove from pan. Cut into small wedges. Serve at room temperature with ice cream or vanilla-sweetened whipped cream, if desired. Serves 10 to 12.

 Enjoy in moderation.

Pena Rivesaultes Rouge (France); Rectorie Banyuls (France).

LENTIL SOUP
SHRIMP ORZO FERRARI
SALMON DE COQUINA
CHICKEN GRISELDA
ROASTED DUCK *with Cherry Sauce*

L a Tour d'Argent opened in 1981 in a picturesque, renovated log cabin and quickly became a Houston favorite for French food, fine wines, hunting lodge décor, polished service and romantic setting (three tables have even earned the title of proposal tables).

Cares recede as you enjoy a drink or glass of wine by the fireplace or dine leisurely in a quiet dining room, cozy nook or at a secluded table. Whenever you need to impress guests — for business meetings, private parties, special occasions and wine dinners — La Tour is a prime choice.

The restaurant is located on White Oak Bayou whose wooded banks provide an ever-changing view of the seasons; the building seems an integral part of the setting. The log cabin, built in 1917, is said to be the oldest in Harris County. It was moved to its present location, but burned just before the opening. Co-owner Sonny Lahham, his wife and several friends scraped and renovated the burned logs, one by one, and the restaurant opened only slightly off schedule.

Lahham built several additions himself including an elegant dining room. He also built the most recent addition, the Bayou Room, which seats 10 and has its special view of the grounds.

The restaurant's 2,000 or more hunting trophies (including tiger skins and rhinoceros heads) and rustic stone fireplaces contrast with elegant leaded glass doors and windows, luxurious antiques, master paintings, chandeliers and fine china. Co-owner Giancarlo Cavatore haunts auctions, art galleries, exhibits and antique shops for art works and fountains that give La Tour d'Argent character. A cast iron fountain of Bacchus that Cavatore found in Greece is a recent addition.

Chef and catering director Hessni Malla, who specializes in classic French cooking and wild game, joined La Tour in 1989. He trained in Europe, worked for several luxury hotels here as well as opening the former Biscayne Restaurant and owning his own restaurant, the Vendome.

Menus focus on French traditions such as pâte, caviar, bouillabaisse, quenelles, chateaubriand, duck, escargots, sweetbreads and rack of lamb. Recent creative additions to the menu include Roquefort and goat cheese soufflés and Grilled Quail Salad with Hazelnut Dressing. Malla is happy to meet special diet requests and because he uses the natural juices instead of flour or roux in sauces, many of the dishes are heart-healthy.

———— *LITE FARE* ————

The classic French cuisine at La Tour d'Argent features lean meats — veal, fish and chicken — accompanied by tasty sauces. To lower fat and sodium, ask for sauces to be served on the side. Daily specials are available that are low in calories, fat and cholesterol. Special requests are encouraged.

La Tour d'Argent
2011 Ella Blvd.
Houston, Tx 77008
713-864-9864

LENTIL SOUP

1	pound lentils
4	teaspoons extra-virgin olive oil
1	medium onion, chopped
4	garlic cloves, diced
8	cups chicken broth
1	bunch cilantro, chopped leaves
2	teaspoons sherry vinegar
	Salt and freshly ground black pepper to taste

Wash and clean lentils thoroughly. Heat oil in medium stockpot; sauté onion and garlic until golden. Add lentils and broth; simmer over medium-low heat until tender, about 45 minutes. Add cilantro, vinegar, salt and pepper. Serves 8.

This is a great low-fat recipe (16 percent calories from fat) and high in fiber (14 grams). Use low-sodium chicken broth.

Enjoy without wine.

SHRIMP ORZO FERRARI

1	cup orzo (rice-shaped pasta)
4	tablespoons clarified margarine
1	medium onion, sliced
4	garlic cloves, diced
1/2	cup sun-dried tomatoes, julienned
1/4	cup salted pistachios
4	teaspoons extra-virgin olive oil
2	teaspoons rice wine vinegar
10	(16/20 count) shrimp, peeled, deveined and cooked
	Fresh thyme leaves
	Salt and freshly ground black pepper to taste
	Endive for garnish
	Sliced hard-cooked egg or sliced tomato for garnish (optional)

Cook orzo in boiling salted water until al dente, about 7 to 8 minutes. Drain and place pasta in large bowl. Heat margarine in small skillet; add onion and garlic. Cook over medium heat until onions are caramelized. Stir into pasta along with tomatoes and pistachios. Add oil, vinegar and shrimp; blend. Season with thyme, salt and pepper. Mix gently and chill covered in refrigerator about 2 hours.

To serve, arrange endive on 2 plates and mound orzo salad on top. Garnish as desired. Serves 2.

Reduce margarine to 2 tablespoons for sautéing. Eliminate oil.

Mirassou Pinot Blanc/White Burgundy; Ferrari Carano Chardonnay or Jordan Chardonnay.

SALMON DE COQUINA

Coquina Salsa (recipe follows)
Assortment of cooked fresh
vegetables for garnish
4   (6- to 8-ounce) salmon fillets

Prepare Coquina Salsa; reserve. Prepare fresh vegetables: slice, carve and cook tender-crisp. Include snow peas, potatoes, yellow squash, zucchini and cherry tomatoes sprinkled with Provencal seasonings. Grill or sauté salmon.

To serve, arrange salmon on lower half of individual plates and top with Coquina Salsa. Fan vegetable garnish above salmon. Serves 4.

COQUINA SALSA

2   ears corn
1   cup peeled, diced, seedless cucumber
1   pink, firm tomato, peeled, seeded and diced
1   medium-size green bell pepper, diced
1   medium-size red bell pepper, diced
1/2 cup diced celery
4   teaspoons fresh lime juice
1   tablespoon extra-virgin olive oil
    Salt and freshly ground black pepper to taste

Coquina Salsa

Cook corn in boiling water until tender; cool and remove kernels. Combine 2 cups kernels, cucumber, tomato, bell peppers, celery, lime juice and oil in a medium glass bowl. Season with salt and pepper.

Salmon is a good source of omega 3 fats that are good for lowering cholesterol. The salsa is low in fat and sodium. Enjoy this tasty and healthful dish.

Saintsbury Pinot Noir (a little over $10); Domaine de Fissey Mercurey (France).

CHICKEN GRISELDA

4   teaspoons extra-virgin olive oil
2   pounds boneless, skinless chicken breasts
1   medium onion, chopped
2   cups sliced mushrooms
1/2 teaspoon grated fresh ginger or 1/8 teaspoon ground powder
1/2 teaspoon dried oregano
1/2 cup dry white wine
2   medium-size green bell peppers, chopped
1   ripe tomato, peeled, seeded and chopped
3   cups chicken broth
    Salt and freshly ground black pepper to taste
3   cups hot cooked rice

Heat oil in large skillet over medium heat; sauté chicken on each side about 2 minutes. Add onion, mushrooms, ginger and oregano. Add wine; simmer until reduced by half. Add peppers, tomato and broth; cook 10 minutes, or until reduced by half. Season with salt and pepper. To serve, place rice in center of plate and surround with sliced chicken. Accompany with mixed green salad. Serves 4.

Use low-sodium chicken broth. This is a healthy low-fat dish. Enjoy!

Fleur du Cap Pinotage (South Africa); Joquet Chinon (France).

ROASTED DUCK *with Cherry Sauce*

1   (4-to-5-pound) duck
    Salt and freshly ground white
    and black peppers to taste,
    divided
1   apple, cut into 2x2-inch squares
1   orange, cut into 2x2-inch
    squares
1   yellow onion, cut into 2x2-inch
    squares
    Olive oil
1/2 teaspoon fresh rosemary leaves
    Cherry Sauce (recipe follows)

Preheat oven to 350 degrees. Sprinkle inside of duck with salt and peppers. Combine apple, orange and onion in medium bowl; stuff duck with mixture. Brush oil over duck; sprinkle with salt, peppers and rosemary. Roast in shallow pan about 3 1/2 hours, turning duck every 30 minutes and basting with drippings.

Prepare Cherry Sauce. When duck is done, remove stuffing. Debone duck and serve with sauce and wild rice. Serves 2.

CHERRY SAUCE

3   teaspoons butter
5   teaspoons brown sugar
2   teaspoons orange zest
1   cup pitted fresh dark petite
    cherries including juice
1/2 cup fresh orange juice
4   teaspoons kirsch (clear cherry
    brandy)
2   teaspoons Grand Marnier

Cherry Sauce

Heat butter and sugar in medium saucepan until softened. Add zest and cook 1 minute, until mixture turns golden. Add cherries and juice. Cook over medium heat until thickened. Add orange juice, kirsch and Grand Marnier. Do not overcook cherries. If sauce is too watery, remove cherries and whisk in 1/2 teaspoon cornstarch dissolved in Grand Marnier to thicken sauce. Return cherries to hot mixture.

Eliminate oil and remove skin from duck before eating. Plenty for 4 servings. This is a great low-fat and low-sodium sauce.

Napa Ridge Pinot Noir; Au Bon Climat Pinot Noir; any top quality red Burgundy from the Côte d'Nuits (France).

GRILLED CORN CHOWDER WITH RED POTATOES AND THYME
CORN RISOTTO
TWICE BAKED POTATOES
MOLASSES AND HONEY ROASTED PORK TENDERLOIN
with Caramelized Onion Balsamic Vinegar Sauce

You might never guess you were eating home cooking at Mark's, but the frequent appearance of corn, sweet potatoes, pork, mashed potatoes and greens on the menu traces back to chef Mark Cox's early days in Wheeling, West Virginia.

Some specialties, such as Mom's Potato Salad, are straight from the originals. But Cox is always on the lookout for unusual ingredients and techniques to put his own stamp on what he calls Progressive American

Cuisine. He buys pulverized corncobs from Colorado to use in smoking, tracked down dried corn from Russia to use in corn crusts for seafood and extracts the juice of the corn to create Corn Risotto.

Suppliers and customers often bring him unique items — a new type of tomato, chile or salad greens, and recently, slats from old white oak barrels. The barrels are originally from the Jack Daniel's Distillery and are used by the McIlhenny family at Avery Island, Louisiana, to brine Tabasco peppers. A good customer, Steve Allen, who supplies cayenne peppers that are brined at Tabasco occasionally brings Cox the slats. They impart distinctive flavors to anything cooked over them.

A meat-and-potatoes kid who grew up on a farm, Cox started his career as a popcorn boy for the Oglebay Park concessions vendor in Wheeling when he was 12. A special task every Wednesday was to pop 500 boxes of corn to sell at the outdoor amphitheater. He decided he wanted to make cooking his career and later went to the Culinary Institute of America at Hyde Park, New York.

After the C.I.A. he apprenticed at the Greenbrier in White Sulphur Springs W. Va., then joined the Four Seasons Hotel in Washington, D.C. He came to Houston to be closer to his future wife, Lisa, and later was executive chef at Brennan's and corporate chef for Tony Vallone's restaurants here.

Mark's opened in July, 1997, in what was originally a small church. Architect Randall Walker and artisan painter David Fernalld transformed the old building. But Gothic elements of the church such as the vaulted ceiling and peaked arch windows remain. An arched glass panel over the bar is etched with a sun face above a midnight blue "sky" studded with gold stars. Fernalld used a Renaissance technique of layering to create custom painted walls of butternut squash yellow, burnt orange and aquamarine.

LITE FARE

The food at Mark's is light, flavorful and fresh. Chef Mark Cox uses fat and sodium sparingly and only in ways that will enhance the taste of the recipe. Since everything is prepared to order, special requests are welcome and encouraged. Seasonal foods are featured on nightly specials.

Mark's
1658 Westheimer
Houston, Tx 77006
713-523-3800

GRILLED CORN CHOWDER WITH RED POTATOES AND THYME

4 ounces apple-smoked bacon, medium diced
1 tablespoon finely chopped garlic
1 cup medium-diced yellow onion
1 cup medium-diced celery
1 cup medium-diced small new red potatoes
3 cups chicken broth
2 cups fresh corn kernels, divided
2 cups whipping cream
1 tablespoon fresh lime juice
1 tablespoon fresh thyme leaves
   Salt and freshly ground white pepper to taste
1/2 tablespoon unsalted butter
2 tablespoons thinly sliced fresh chives

Sauté bacon in a medium saucepan over medium heat until crispy and golden brown. Remove bacon; reserve. Add garlic, onion and celery to bacon drippings. Stirring occasionally, sauté 5 minutes. Add potatoes and broth; bring to a boil, reduce heat and simmer uncovered 5 minutes.

Preheat oven to 350 degrees. Lightly pulse 1 1/3 cups corn in food processor or dice by hand. Add to potato mixture; simmer 5 minutes. Stir in cream, bring to a boil; reduce heat and simmer 7 minutes, or until thickened to the consistency of cream. Remove from heat; stir in lime juice, thyme, reserved bacon, salt and pepper.

Melt butter until golden in a non-stick ovenproof skillet over medium heat. Add remaining 2/3 cup corn, stir and season to taste with salt and pepper. Roast in oven 7 to 10 minutes or until a rich golden brown, stirring as needed. Remove and reserve.

To serve, ladle chowder into tureen or individual soup bowls. Garnish with roasted corn and chives. Serves 4.

Reduce bacon to 2 ounces. Use low-sodium chicken broth. Substitute evaporated skim milk for cream.

Fetzer Gewürztraminer; Schoffit Tokay Pinot Gris (France).

CORN RISOTTO

4	ears corn, kernels removed, divided
6	tablespoons unsalted butter, divided
1	tablespoon olive oil
1/4	cup finely minced yellow onion
1	cup Arborio rice
4	cups chicken broth, divided
	Salt and freshly ground white pepper to taste
1	teaspoon sugar
1/4	cup freshly grated Parmigiano-Reggiano cheese
1	red bell pepper, roasted
1	yellow bell pepper, roasted
24	sugar snap peas

Preheat oven to 350 degrees. Reserve one-fourth of corn for garnish. Put remaining three-fourths of corn through juice extractor (preferably) or blender; reserve.

Heat 1 tablespoon butter and oil in a medium skillet over medium heat. Stir in onion; cook 3 to 4 minutes. Add rice; stir to coat rice. Add extracted corn juice and broth one ladle at a time; cook until liquid is absorbed into rice.

Brown remaining corn in 1 tablespoon butter in a small ovenproof skillet; add sugar. Roast in oven 7 to 10 minutes or until golden brown, stirring as needed. Remove and reserve.

Stir remaining 4 tablespoons butter into risotto; garnish with Parmesan. Reheat peppers and corn. Cook peas in a small amount of salted water until tender-crisp, about 1 minute. Place risotto in serving bowl; garnish with julienned roasted peppers and corn. Top with peas. Serves 8.

 Reduce butter to 2 tablespoons. Substitute low-sodium chicken broth.

Chateau de Cheylane Rosé (France); Commanderie de Peyrassol Rosé (France) or Bruno Giacosa Bruit Rosé Sparkling Wine (Italy).

TWICE BAKED POTATOES

3	large Idaho baking potatoes
6	florets fresh broccoli
6	florets fresh cauliflower
1 1/2	cups shredded white Cheddar cheese
6	tablespoons sliced green onions
3/4	cup sour cream
3	tablespoons unsalted butter
	Worcestershire and hot pepper sauce to taste
	Salt and freshly ground black pepper to taste

Preheat oven to 400 degrees. Bake potatoes until tender, about 45 minutes to 1 hour. Cook broccoli and cauliflower florets in lightly salted water until tender. Remove from water; plunge into ice water to stop cooking process; drain and reserve.

Slice baked potatoes in half lengthwise. Remove pulp of potato, leaving shell intact. Reserve shells. Put potato pulp, broccoli, cauliflower, cheese, onion, sour cream and butter into medium mixing bowl. Stir until chunky. Season with Worcestershire, pepper sauce, salt and pepper. Restuff potato shells, mounding stuffing over the top. Can be made ahead and refrigerated.

To serve, reheat in 350-degree oven 10 to 15 minutes, or if made ahead 20 minutes. Serve with Molasses and Honey Roasted Pork Tenderloin. Serves 6.

 Reduce cheese to 1/2 cup. Substitute light sour cream for regular and reduce to 1/2 cup. Reduce butter to 1 tablespoon.

MOLASSES AND HONEY ROASTED PORK TENDERLOIN
with *Caramelized Balsamic Vinegar Sauce*

Caramelized Balsamic Vinegar
Sauce (recipe follows)
2 vacuum-packed boneless pork
tenderloins (2 pounds total)
Salt and freshly ground black
pepper to taste
1/4 cup olive oil
1/2 cup honey
1/4 cup unsulphured molasses
Twice Baked Potatoes (recipe
precedes)

**CARAMELIZED BALSAMIC
VINEGAR SAUCE**

1 1/2 cups medium-diced red onion
1 tablespoon unsalted butter
2/3 cup red wine vinegar
1/2 cup balsamic vinegar
1 cup chicken broth

Prepare Caramelized Balsamic Vinegar Sauce. Preheat oven to 400 degrees. Remove any silver skin and excess fat from tenderloin; season with salt and pepper. Heat oil in large skillet over high heat; lightly sear tenderloins evenly on all sides.

Combine honey and molasses in small bowl; brush tenderloin with mixture. Bake in oven 8 to 10 minutes, or until done. Remove from oven and slice into 1/2-inch thick medallions. Fan medallions out in a semi-circle on plate around a Twice Baked Potato. At each side put a small amount of caramelized onions from sauce. Pour Caramelized Balsamic Vinegar Sauce over pork. Serves 4 (1/2 tender per person).

Caramelized Balsamic Vinegar Sauce

Sauté onion in butter over medium heat in medium saucepan until golden brown. Add wine vinegar, balsamic vinegar and broth; bring to a boil. Reduce heat and simmer 15 minutes.

Caramelized Balsamic Vinegar Sauce: Reduce butter to 1/2 tablespoon. Use low-sodium chicken broth. Reduce oil to 2 tablespoons to sear meat. Pork tenderloin is a lean meat and this recipe is healthy and low fat. To stay within the American Heart Association recommendation of 6 ounces or less of meat per day, stretch this recipe to 6 servings.

Cline Zinfandel; Ravenswood Zinfandel or De Loach Zinfandel.

FACING PAGE, FROM LEFT: *Lisa and Mark Cox, Mark's.*

FOLLOWING PAGE, FROM LEFT: *Alice Vongvisith, Nit Noi; Charles Dash, St. Regis.*

ALICE'S CHICKEN DELIGHT
CABBAGE SOUP
CRISPY RED SNAPPER
THAI STICKY RICE *with Thai Custard* AND MANGO

In the past 20 years Houston has taken a shine to Thai food. And Nit Noi, with three locations, has made a big impression on our taste buds. Many regulars go two or three times a week to satisfy their appetites for the cuisine of owner Alice Vongvisith's homeland. She grew up in Korat, the center of rice noodle manufacturing in Thailand where the best (the thinnest) noodles come from, she says.

Typical dishes include a Nit Noi favorite, Putt-Thai, which in Korat would be made with beef, chicken or pork — not shrimp — an assortment of vegetables, eggs and bean sprouts. Korat also is a rice- and vegetable-growing area so creations such as Alice's Delight include mixtures of vegetables. She often adds a fruit accent because tropical fruits also were grown in Korat. Other menu items representative of her "home cooking" are Curry Chicken and Cabbage Soup.

She comes from a large and virtually self-sufficient family — they had their own rice, fruit and fish farms. Alice always liked to cook but never did so professionally until she had a restaurant in the Philippines before moving to the United States.

Thai cuisine is traditionally a balance of five flavors — hot, bitter, sweet, sour and salty. Alice seems to have an intrinsic understanding of what each ingredient contributes to a dish, especially vegetable dishes.

"People seem to be ordering more vegetable (and vegetarian) dishes in the past five years." And on recent trips to Thailand she noticed many more people have become vegetarians, she said. One of the most popular recent additions is Musmun, named for a Thai herb seasoning paste. The dish is a mixture of sliced Kabocha squash (which look like miniature pumpkins), roasted peanuts, musmun, Thai curry, chilies and Roma tomatoes.

Alice is known as a sharp businesswoman, but one who is interested in making the business an art as well as a success. She greets most customers with warm recognition and a hug. Evenings and weekends, her husband, Sam, an engineer at Kellogg and Co., is on hand. Their daughter-in-law Melisa manages the Rice Village location on Bolsover and Alice's son, Doi Heckler, the new restaurant on Woodway.

*Nit Noi
2462 Bolsover
5211 Kelvin
Houston, Tx 77005
713-524-8114*

*6395 Woodway
Houston, Tx 77057
713-789-1711*

——————— *LITE FARE* ———————

Thai cuisine is generally light and healthy if you skirt the fried items. Rice and lots of veggies keep the carbohydrate content high. The Nit Noi menu offers an extensive selection of vegetarian dishes. Some of the stir-fried dishes can be prepared oil-free. Request sauces to be served on the side.

ALICE'S CHICKEN DELIGHT

1   cup brown rice
1/2 cup wild rice
2   (4-ounce) boneless, skinless
     chicken breast halves
1   egg
1   tablespoon soy sauce
1/2 teaspoon sugar
1/2 teaspoon freshly ground black
     pepper
6   pineapple chunks
1/2 bunch broccoli, broken into
     florets
1/2 cup sliced carrots
1/2 cup sliced asparagus
1/2 cup sliced yellow squash
1/2 cup snow peas
2   tablespoons vegetable oil
1/2 tablespoon finely chopped garlic
2   tablespoons oyster sauce
1/2 tablespoon Thai fish sauce
     (nam pla)

Cook brown and wild rice together according to brown rice package directions; reserve. Cut chicken into 15 bite-size cubes. Combine egg, soy sauce, sugar and pepper in medium bowl. Add chicken and pineapple; marinate 10 minutes.

Skewer 5 pieces of chicken between 2 pineapple chunks on an 8-inch skewer. Repeat with 2 more skewers. Grill skewers about 7 minutes, or until chicken is cooked.

Drop broccoli, carrots, asparagus and squash into rapidly boiling water and blanch 1 minute; drain and immediately plunge into ice water to stop cooking. Drain well on paper towels. Heat oil in skillet; sauté broccoli, carrots, asparagus, squash, snow peas and garlic. Stir in oyster sauce and fish sauce. Add rice to mixture; stir.

Place vegetable rice mixture on platter and arrange skewers of chicken on top. Serves 3.

Great low-fat recipe. Use low-sodium soy sauce.

Fall Creek Chenin Blanc (Texas); Chappellet Old Vine Cuvée.

CABBAGE SOUP

1	(3-to-4-pound) chicken
6	cups chicken broth (from chicken or canned)
1	head Chinese cabbage, slice into bite-size pieces
1	pound firm tofu, cut into bite-size squares
2	teaspoons fish sauce (Shrimp brand recommended)
1/2	bunch cilantro (leaves only), chopped
	Freshly ground black pepper to taste
4	ounces clear rice noodles (sticks)
4	teaspoons chopped garlic, sautéed until golden

Clean chicken, remove giblets (reserve for another use) and place chicken in large stockpot; add water to cover. Bring water to a boil; reduce heat and simmer, covered, until chicken is tender, 2 1/2 to 3 hours. Remove chicken; save broth. Add canned broth, if necessary, to reserved broth to measure 6 cups.

Skin and bone chicken; cut meat into bite-size pieces. Return chicken to pot; add broth, cabbage, tofu, fish sauce, cilantro and pepper. Soak noodles in cold water 10 minutes, drain and add to broth. Bring soup to a boil and add garlic. Serve immediately. Serves 6.

🍎 Cool chicken broth and skim off fat before using or use a fat-free, low-sodium canned chicken broth.

🍇 Enjoy without wine.

CRISPY RED SNAPPER

3	medium tomatoes, cut in chunks
2	tablespoons pineapple chunks (fresh or canned)
1/2	cup finely chopped straw mushrooms
	Peanut oil or vegetable oil
1	whole head garlic, peeled and chopped
3	Thai chili peppers
2	tablespoons Thai fish sauce (nam pla)
2	tablespoons oyster sauce
2	tablespoons sugar
2	chicken bouillon cubes or 2 teaspoons bouillon granules
1/2	cup white wine
1	egg white
1	tablespoon cornstarch
3	(8-ounce) snapper fillets
3 to 4	basil leaves, chopped, plus more whole leaves for garnish

Coarsely chop tomatoes, pineapple and mushrooms in food processor. Heat 2 tablespoons oil in hot skillet. Blend garlic and chilies in skillet; stir until garlic releases its aroma. Add tomato mixture to skillet; stir until well blended. Add fish sauce, oyster sauce, sugar, bouillon and wine. Cook, stirring, until sauce comes to a boil. Reduce heat and simmer about 10 minutes, or until sauce cooks down and thickens as desired.

Mix egg white and cornstarch until well blended. Meanwhile, in another skillet, heat additional oil for frying; heat until almost smoking. Dip each fillet in egg mixture and fry in oil. Drain. Place each fillet on plate. Add basil to sauce and divide sauce among fillets. Garnish with basil leaves. Serve with steamed rice. Serves 2 to 3.

🍎 This is a great low-fat recipe. To reduce sodium, use low-sodium chicken broth and reduce fish and oyster sauces to 1 tablespoon each.

🍇 Rosemount Chardonnay (Australia); Penfold's "The Valleys" Chardonnay (Australia) or Clos Pegase "Mitsuko's" Chardonnay.

THAI STICKY RICE *with Thai Custard* AND MANGO

Thai Custard (recipe follows)
2 **cups cooked sticky (glutinous) rice**
1 **(14-ounce) can coconut milk (Chaokoh brand recommended), divided**
1 **mango**
Strawberries for garnish

Sticky glutinous rice is available in Asian food markets, Fiesta and other food specialty-import shops, and it must be steamed on a rack over simmering water, not boiled. At Nit Noi, Thai purple rice is frequently used and it must be soaked for two days.

Prepare Thai Custard; refrigerate until needed. If using imported Thai rice, soak in water overnight (or follow package directions for soaking). Drain water off, place rice in a steamer rack over simmering water and steam until cooked. When cooked, mix with 1 cup coconut milk to make the mixture creamy (see Notes).

Just before serving, peel and slice mango. To serve: Arrange rice in a mound in center of a dessert dish. Spoon custard over it and top with mango slices. Garnish with strawberries. Serves 4.

Notes: Do not shake can. Spoon the thickened creamy milk from the top of the can into a 1-cup measure.

As an alternative, jasmine rice may be used. A quick home method is to prepare this in the microwave. Place 1 cup jasmine rice in a 1 1/2-quart microwave dish. Add water to 1/2-inch depth above rice; stir. Microwave uncovered on high 5 minutes. Stir; cover with lid and microwave on high 4 to 5 more minutes. Stir with fork.

THAI CUSTARD

2 **eggs**
1/4 **cup brown sugar**
Dash of salt
1/2 **cup coconut milk from 14-ounce can**
1 **apple, such as Red or Golden Delicious, peeled, seeded and chopped**

Thai Custard

Place eggs, sugar, salt, milk and apple in blender; process until smooth. Pour into round bowl or dish. Bring water to a boil in a pan with steamer rack. Place dish on rack, reduce heat, cover pan and steam over simmering water 30 to 45 minutes, until thick and firm when tested with a knife inserted in the center. Remove from steamer; let cool, then refrigerate until needed.

🍎 Coconut milk is high in total fat and saturated fat. Use moderation with this dessert.

🍇 Gratien and Meyer Cuvée Delice (France); Commanderia St. John (Cypress).

LAMB ENCHILADAS
CORN CRUSTED REDFISH *with Cilantro Avocado Sauce*
BAKED ALASKA

P ost Oak Grill is a combination of influence from its owners and chef — Ethel Fisher, third-generation Houstonian and fourth-generation Texan; Manfred Jachmich, classically trained in Europe; and chef Polo Becerra, from Mexico. Their diverse backgrounds combine in an eclectic menu with dishes that often blend elements of Old World, New World and regional favorites. Fisher and Jachmich also own a Post Oak Grill in Beaumont and are planning a third Grill in the Tunnel downtown under 1111 Louisiana.

When Fisher was about 10, she took orders for cakes in the neighborhood to earn money to ride horses in Memorial Park. She delighted in working her way through the Time-Life series of cookbooks and later polished her French cooking techniques during summer trips to the South of France.

Jachmich has been involved with several well-known Houston restaurants including Ruggles. He comes from a restaurant family in Koblenz, Germany, where he trained as a pastry chef. He brings continental flair to the menus and is known for time-honored specialties including Trout Manfred, Tomatoes Manfred, Wienerschnitzel and English Trifle.

Becerra, who grew up as one of eight children on a vegetable farm in Mexico, sold vegetables every Sunday in the village market. He and a brother also made goat and cow's milk cheeses. (One brother is now mayor of Puerto Vallarta). Polo graduated from Conalep culinary school. He joined Post Oak Grill in 1989 and by 1994 had moved up from cook to sous chef to executive chef. He has a special talent for seafood and vegetables and enjoys satisfying customers' special requests.

Recent menu additions explore new territory — corn-crusted redfish is dressed with Cilantro Avocado Sauce; fresh tuna is pan-seared and served with sesame sautéed spinach and wild rice cake; an American buffalo burger is grilled to order. Post Oak Grill also is known for luscious cookies and desserts.

The restaurant is a neighborhood gathering place for lunch, a drink after work or a workout, dinner-for-two or family birthday. It is known for appealing ambiance - garlands of lights entwined in grapevines stretch across the ceiling. The glass-enclosed atrium, Wine Room, Board Room and piano bar, which offers dancing six nights a week to live music, attract a wide variety of patrons.

LITE FARE

Post Oak Grill uses a star to designate dishes prepared in a lighter style. Try the Balsamic Angel Hair—a tasty entrée of angel hair pasta with roasted chicken, Roma tomatoes and exotic mushrooms sautéed in a fat-free garlic balsamic vinegar. Other light entrées include grilled shrimp, grilled trout and pan-seared tuna.

Post Oak Grill
1415 S. Post Oak Lane
Houston, Tx 77056
713-993-9966

LAMB ENCHILADAS

3   cups Enchilada Sauce (recipe follows)
1 1/2   pounds lamb loin, cut into 1/4-inch cubes
1   small yellow onion, diced
4   Roma tomatoes, diced
1 1/2   green bell peppers, diced
2   tablespoons extra-virgin olive oil, divided
1   tablespoon soy sauce
    Salt and freshly ground black pepper to taste
3   tablespoons freshly grated imported Parmesan cheese
2   tablespoons chopped chives
1   tablespoon chopped fresh oregano
1   tablespoon chopped cilantro leaves
12   (6-inch) corn tortillas
1/2   pound crumbled goat cheese (preferably French)
1   cup sour cream
12   mint leaves

ENCHILADA SAUCE

1   tablespoon olive oil
2   guajillo chilies (dried dark red-black chilies) or anchos, seeded
4   pasilla chilies (chile negro), seeded
4   garlic cloves
1/4   medium-size yellow onion
3   (6-inch) corn tortillas, cut into quarters
6   cups vegetable broth
1   tablespoon chopped fresh mint
    Salt and freshly ground black pepper to taste

Prepare Enchilada Sauce; reserve. (Refrigerate covered if not used immediately.) Sauté lamb cubes, onion, tomatoes and bell pepper in a very hot skillet with 1 tablespoon oil 4 minutes. Add soy sauce, salt and pepper to taste.

Combine Parmesan, chives, oregano and cilantro in small bowl; reserve. In another skillet, soften tortillas in remaining 1 tablespoon oil, using more if necessary. Drain tortillas on paper towel. Divide lamb mixture and place in center of each tortilla; divide herb mixture and place on top of lamb mixture of each tortilla. Roll tortillas.

Pour a layer of Enchilada Sauce on each of 6 plates; top with 2 enchiladas seam side down. Garnish each plate with goat cheese, dollop of sour cream and 2 mint leaves. Serves 6.

Enchilada Sauce

Heat oil in medium nonstick skillet; fry chilies over medium-high heat 1 minute. Add garlic, onion and tortillas; fry 2 minutes. Put mixture into food processor along with broth; puree. Return sauce to skillet, add mint and cook over medium-high heat until reduced by one-third. Season with salt and pepper. Cover and refrigerate extra for future use. Makes 4 cups.

Eliminate oil for softening tortillas and warm tortillas in the microwave by wrapping 6 tortillas in a damp paper towel; microwave on high 45 seconds. Reduce goat cheese to 1/4 pound. Substitute reduced-fat sour cream for regular and reduce amount to 1 tablespoon per serving. Use low-sodium vegetable broth in Enchilada Sauce. Great low-fat sauce.

Rosemount Shiraz (Australia); McDowell Valley Syrah or Zaca Mesa Syrah; Diamond Creek or Silver Oak Cabernet Sauvignon.

CORN CRUSTED REDFISH
with Cilantro Avocado Sauce

Cilantro Avocado Sauce (recipe follows)
2/3 cup olive oil
3 tablespoons finely chopped garlic
1 tablespoon fresh chopped oregano
1 tablespoon fresh chopped basil
1 tablespoon fresh chopped thyme
Salt and freshly ground black pepper to taste
6 (7-ounce) redfish fillets
3 cups fresh corn kernels, cut from cob
3 tablespoons fresh chopped parsley
5 eggs
2/3 cup all-purpose flour
2/3 cup clarified unsalted butter, divided (see Special Helps section)

CILANTRO AVOCADO SAUCE

2 avocados, seeded and peeled
1 (14 1/2-ounce) can heated chicken broth, divided
1/2 cup chopped cilantro leaves
1 jalapeño, seeded and cut into 6 pieces
2 tablespoons fresh lime juice
Salt and freshly ground black pepper to taste

Prepare Cilantro Avocado Sauce; reserve. Combine oil, garlic, oregano, basil, thyme, salt and pepper in medium bowl. Marinate fillets in mixture 15 minutes.

Combine corn and parsley in medium bowl; set aside. Beat eggs in small bowl. Place flour in flat pan. Dredge fillet through flour on one side; then coat both sides of fillet with egg. Press floured side of fillet into corn mixture, pressing down firmly. Repeat with remaining fillets.

Heat 1/3 cup butter in medium skillet until very hot. Sauté 3 fillets at a time, corn side down, 3 minutes. Flip to other side and sauté 3 minutes. Reduce temperature to low, cover pan and cook 5 to 7 minutes. Turn fillets again and increase temperature to brown corn crust, 2 to 3 minutes. Repeat process for remaining 3 fillets. Serve with Cilantro Avocado Sauce. Serves 6.

An easy alternative method is to sauté fish on both sides, arrange on a baking sheet and place in a preheated 400-degree oven 10 to 12 minutes. Finish under broiler for browning.

Cilantro Avocado Sauce

Place avocados, half of broth, cilantro, jalapeño, lime juice, salt and pepper in blender; puree. Adjust seasoning and add enough of the remaining broth to achieve a creamy consistency.

Eliminate oil in marinade and rub fish fillets with garlic and herbs. Substitute 2 whole eggs and 6 egg whites for 5 whole eggs. Use 2 tablespoons of Cilantro Avocado Sauce per fillet. Use low-sodium chicken broth in Cilantro Avocado Sauce.

Napa Ridge Chardonnay; J.J. Vincent St. Veran (France) or De Wetshof Chardonnay (South Africa); Kistler or Far Niente Chardonnay.

BAKED ALASKA

2 (1-pound) Sara Lee pound cakes
1 pint cinnamon ice cream (see Note)
3/4 cup chocolate syrup, divided
1 cup toasted chopped pecans, divided
1 pint Kahlua ice cream
1 pint chocolate ice cream
6 egg whites
Pinch of salt
1 cup sugar, divided

Day before: Cut each cake into 5 slices lengthwise with a serrated knife. Line a 2-quart metal bowl with plastic wrap or wax paper. Arrange slices of cake around sides and bottom of bowl (may need to trim slices to fit bottom).

Soften cinnamon ice cream slightly in medium bowl; beat with portable mixer on low speed just until smooth. Do not let melt. Pour on top of cake; pour half of chocolate sauce over ice cream and top with 1/2 cup pecans. Freeze about 30 minutes.

Repeat softening process with Kahlua ice cream; add to previous layer along with remaining chocolate sauce and pecans. Return to freezer.

Repeat softening process with chocolate ice cream; add to previous layer. Top with remaining cake slices; cover with plastic wrap and freeze overnight.

Preheat oven to 500 degrees. Beat egg whites with salt until they hold soft peaks. Beat in sugar, 2 tablespoons at a time, until meringue is stiff and shiny. Place a piece of aluminum foil on cookie sheet, remove plastic wrap from cake and turn cake onto a cookie sheet. Spread meringue over entire ice cream cake. Bake on middle rack in oven until meringue is golden, about 4 to 5 minutes: watch carefully. Slide Baked Alaska onto serving platter using a wide spatula. Pull foil away; serve immediately. Serves 8.

Note: Cinnamon ice cream is available at some ice cream shops. To make your own, slightly soften 1 pint vanilla ice cream in medium bowl and stir in 1 tablespoon ground cinnamon and proceed as directed. Other ice cream flavors may be used.

Substitute low-fat ice cream for regular.

 Enjoy without wine.

SHELLY'S SALAD
CHILLED JUMBO SHRIMP *with Jalapeño Remoulade*
BEER CHEESE SOUP
JALAPEÑO CORN MUFFINS
MIXED BERRY COBBLER

Redwood Grill is a showcase for fine-tuned American cuisine. The creative use of fresh herbs, cheeses and sauces glamorizes basic chicken, shrimp, vegetables and pasta. Owned by Manfred Jachmich and Ethel Fisher, the Grill draws a lunch crowd from downtown, the Montrose area, Museum District and Medical Center. The restaurant, which seats 160 and is a nonsmoking facility, is a convenient place to congregate before or after the theater. Grapevines wreathed with lights over the tables, terra cotta walls, dark woods and upholstered booths create inviting surroundings. The Bombay Private Dining Room accommodates private parties and the chef's periodic cooking classes.

Executive chef Shelly Drought cooks in many languages. Some menu items have a Southwestern or Mexican accent: Jalapeño Fettuccini with Black Beans is topped with grilled chicken. Sometimes the mood

turns Asian — seared tuna is served with bok choy and wasabi-flavored mashed potatoes. A Mediterranean personality emerges in Medallions of Veal Tenderloin with spinach, sun-dried tomatoes, portobello mushrooms and orzo. Roasted garlic, Tequila Lime Salsa, Jalapeño Remoulade, mangos, tomatillos, ginger, wine sauces, pine nuts, candied pecans, roasted walnuts and caramelized onions play a variety of roles.

Cooking may be in Drought's genes. Her mother's family has always been involved in restaurants in San Antonio (her grandfather, who owned B&B Bar-B-Que was known as the "king of barbecue" there, she says.) Shelly has loved cooking since she was about 10; she read cookbooks like some kids read comic books. As the oldest child, she would baby-sit her sister and while their parents were out, she would call the grocery store and have them deliver ingredients. By the time her parents returned she would have a three-course meal ready.

While growing up, she would hang around the cooks in her grandmother's big kitchen, where a party or some food was usually under preparation. Her parents grew vegetables at the family's ranch in the Hill Country and in a garden in town, which gave her an appreciation of fresh, high-quality produce.

"I didn't know there was canned spinach until I was practically grown," she says.

After graduation from the French Culinary Institute, she worked at Gracie Mansion, the New York governor's residence, and in Honolulu and San Antonio, where she helped open Biga restaurant.

LITE FARE

Shelly Drought features some tasty and healthy dishes on the Redwood Grill menu. The snapper comes with a Ginger Tomatillo Salsa, the tuna is served with a lemongrass broth and ginger slaw and the grouper comes in a Habanero Cilantro Broth with diced mangoes. Shelly welcomes and encourages special requests.

Redwood Grill
4611 Montrose Blvd.
Houston, Tx 77006
713-523-4611

SHELLY'S SALAD

1/2 cup Candied Pecans (recipe follows)
1/3 cup Honey Balsamic Vinaigrette (recipe follows)
4 cups field greens or mesclun mix
1 cup crumbled blue cheese
1 Granny Smith apple, cored and julienned

Prepare Candied Pecans; reserve. Prepare Honey Balsamic Vinaigrette; reserve. Combine greens with dressing to lightly coat. Divide greens among 4 chilled salad plates, top each with 1/4 cup cheese, 2 tablespoons Candied Pecans and one-fourth of apple. Serves 4.

CANDIED PECANS

1/4 cup sugar
1/4 cup boiling water
4 cups pecan pieces

Candied Pecans

Preheat oven to 350 degrees. Place sugar in a medium bowl; add boiling water and stir until dissolved. Add pecans; toss in mixture. Pour pecans in a single layer onto a lightly buttered cookie sheet and bake 12 to 15 minutes. Cool and store in an airtight container. Makes 4 cups.

HONEY BALSAMIC VINAIGRETTE

1/2 cup vegetable oil
1/2 cup honey
1/4 cup balsamic vinegar
1/2 tablespoon chopped fresh assorted herbs of choice
1 shallot, chopped
Salt and freshly ground black pepper to taste

Honey Balsamic Vinaigrette

Combine oil, honey, vinegar, herbs and shallot with a whisk in a medium bowl. Season with salt and pepper. Cover and refrigerate extra up to 3 months. Makes 1 cup.

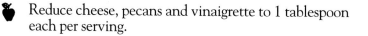 Reduce cheese, pecans and vinaigrette to 1 tablespoon each per serving.

Beringer White Zinfandel; Iron Horse Brut Rosé Sparkling Wine.

CHILLED JUMBO SHRIMP *with Jalapeño Remoulade*

1/2 cup Jalapeño Remoulade (recipe follows)
16 jumbo shrimp, peeled and deveined with tails left intact
Water
2 bay leaves
3 peppercorns
1/2 cup dry white wine
Salt to taste
Chives and paprika for garnish

JALAPEÑO REMOULADE

1 roasted jalapeño, peeled and seeded
1 cup mayonnaise
1/4 cup sour cream
1/2 tablespoon paprika

Prepare Jalapeño Remoulade; cover and refrigerate. Fill a large bowl with ice and water; set aside. Bring enough water to cover shrimp to a boil with bay leaves, peppercorns, wine and salt. Add shrimp, return to a boil and remove from heat; cover and let sit until shrimp turn pink. Remove shrimp and immediately plunge into ice water; remove and drain when shrimp are cold.

Arrange 4 shrimp in each of 4 margarita glasses. Put 2 tablespoons of Jalapeño Remoulade on top; garnish with chives and paprika. Serves 4.

Jalapeño Remoulade

Roast jalapeño on a flat grill until blackened and blistered, about 5 minutes. Leave vent on over range and avoid breathing fumes or handling peppers without gloves. Put pepper into plastic bag; let sit a few minutes until softened and using plastic bag, slip off peel.

Put jalapeño, mayonnaise, sour cream and paprika into blender or food processor; puree until smooth. Makes 1 1/4 cups. Unused portion may be refrigerated as long as 1 week.

🍎 Prepare Jalapeño Remoulade with light mayonnaise and low-fat sour cream.

🍇 Firestone Riesling; Domaine des Baumard Savennieres (France).

BEER CHEESE SOUP

1/4 cup vegetable oil
1 yellow onion, chopped
2 to 3 jalapeños, seeded and chopped
2 garlic cloves, chopped
4 ribs celery, chopped
3 large carrots, chopped
3 (12-ounce) bottles dark beer (Shiner Bock recommended)
1 bunch cilantro, leaves only, chopped
4 cups chicken broth
4 cups whipping cream
5 cups shredded sharp Cheddar cheese

Heat oil in large stockpot; sauté onion, jalapeños, garlic, celery and carrots until softened, about 7 minutes. Add beer and bring to a boil. Add cilantro and broth; return to a boil. Pour in cream, bring to a boil and reduce over medium-high heat until mixture coats the back of a spoon, about 10 minutes.

In batches, puree mixture in blender or food processor until smooth. Return to stockpot and bring to a boil. Reduce heat to low and slowly stir in a handful of cheese at a time with a wire whisk until smooth, about 10 minutes. Never let soup boil again or cheese will burn or separate. Makes 10 (1-cup) servings.

🍎 Reduce oil for sautéing to 2 tablespoons. Use low-sodium, low-fat chicken broth. Substitute evaporated skim milk for cream. Substitute low-fat, low-sodium cheese for regular.

🍇 Mariposa Malbec (Argentina); Foppiano Petite Syrah.

JALAPEÑO CORN MUFFINS

1/2	cup sugar
7	tablespoons water, divided
1 1/2	cups bread flour
3/4	cup yellow cornmeal
6	tablespoons nonfat dry milk
1 1/2	teaspoons baking powder
1/2	teaspoon salt
2	eggs
6	tablespoons vegetable oil
1/2	(12-ounce) can roasted red peppers, drained and chopped
1	(8 3/4-ounce) can whole kernel corn
3	ounces canned pickled jalapeños, drained and chopped

Preheat oven to 350 degrees. Grease muffin pans or spray with nonstick spray; set aside. Beat sugar and 2 tablespoons water in a medium mixing bowl. Add flour, cornmeal, nonfat milk, baking powder and salt; mix until smooth. Gradually beat in eggs, oil and remaining 5 tablespoons water. Add red peppers, corn and jalapeños. Fill each muffin cup three-fourths full. Bake until golden brown, about 15 to 17 minutes. Makes about 18 muffins.

🍎 Great recipe. Enjoy!

MIXED BERRY COBBLER

3 to 4	large muffins or biscuits of choice
1	pint fresh strawberries, sliced
1	pint fresh blueberries
1	pint fresh blackberries
1 1/2	cups sugar, divided
	Juice of 1/2 lemon
2	tablespoons all-purpose flour
1	cup unsalted butter, cubed
1	cup all-purpose flour
1	cup packed brown sugar
1/2	teaspoon ground cinnamon
	Vanilla ice cream
	Powdered sugar for garnish

Preheat oven to 350 degrees or 325 degrees for glass. Butter a 13x9x2-inch pan or glass dish or spray with nonstick spray. Crumble and press muffins in bottom of dish; set aside.

Toss berries with 1 cup sugar and lemon juice in a large bowl. Place berry mixture on top of muffins; sprinkle 2 tablespoons flour over top.

To make topping, put butter, 1 cup flour and brown sugar in food processor or medium mixing bowl. Pulse processor or mix on low speed just until mixture is crumbly. Sprinkle over berries. Combine cinnamon with remaining 1/2 cup sugar and sprinkle over top. Bake 40 to 50 minutes, or until golden. Cut into squares; divide among 12 bowls, top with vanilla ice cream and sprinkle with powdered sugar. Serves 12.

 Substitute low-fat ice cream for regular.

🍇 Nozzole Nivole 1/2 bottle (Italy) or Ballatore Spumante; Santo Stephano Moscato d'Asti (Italy).

STILTON, ENDIVE AND BABY FIELD GREENS *with Spicy Walnuts & Walnut Vinaigrette*
SEARED SEA SCALLOPS *with Red Onion Marmalade*
GRILLED ANGUS FILET MIGNON WITH MUSHROOM, DRIED CRANBERRY RAGOUT
SCALLOPED POTATOES RIVIERA
CRÉME BRÛLÉE RIVIERA

Houston food lovers are constantly surprised to find this fine-dining restaurant in a hotel outside Loop 610. That they will drive miles is a tribute to owner/chef John Sheely and his innovative Mediterranean cuisine.

Recently Sheely has been concentrating more on the cooking of southern France than the Riviera. But signature dishes such as shrimp wrapped in a crisp shell of kataifi, finely shredded filo dough resembling shredded wheat, are still on the menu.

Sheely's family came to Galveston from Milan in the early 1900s. He used to help his great-aunts make ravioli, a two-day process. Interest in food seems to run in the family. His mother formerly was catering

director for a Red Carpet Inn. His brother, Steven, is food and beverage director of Braeburn Country Club, and the Sheelys' two daughters, Delilah and Lisa, work at Riviera. Lisa also is in charge of room service at the Radisson. Sheely is responsible for all the food, room service and catering for the 173-room hotel as well as private parties.

His career started modestly at Burger King when he was at Westchester High School. A self-described "ski bum," Sheely moved to Vail, Colorado after graduation and worked in restaurants to support himself. Later he developed his style at a small restaurant he owned for two years before returning to Houston in 1994.

He and his wife, Alicia, opened Riviera Grill in a strip shopping center outside the Loop, but the location proved difficult and in 1996 Sheely relocated to the Radisson Suite. Loyal fans come for such dishes as Tenderloin of Beef with Sweet Onion Confit and Rack of Lamb with Focaccia Herb Crust and Caponata. And they marvel over such ingenious dishes as mashed potatoes flavored with a reduction of red wine, sweet pea risotto, sun-dried tomato polenta and an appetizer terrine of Stilton cheese, fresh figs, greens and toasted walnuts.

Lunch menus include salads and sandwiches. If Sheely were in charge, mothers would seldom have to admonish us to eat our vegetables. Who wouldn't be intrigued by the Grilled Vegetable Plate served with Crispy Polenta, Arugula Pesto and Toasted Pine Nuts or Wild Mushroom Risotto with Grilled Vegetables and Port Wine Glaze?

--- LITE FARE ---

The Riviera Grill menu gives as much prominence to fresh vegetables, fruits, and grains as it does to meats and seafood. Enjoy the risotto, pastas and grilled vegetables, seasoned to perfection with fresh herbs. Special requests for dietary needs will be accommodated. Dressings and sauces can be served on the side.

Riviera Grill
Radisson Suite Hotel
10655 Katy Freeway
Houston, Tx 77024
713-974-4445

STILTON, ENDIVE AND BABY FIELD GREENS
with Spicy Walnuts & Walnut Vinaigrette

Spicy Walnuts (recipe follows)
Walnut Vinaigrette (recipe follows)
4   cups mixed field greens
1   cup crumbled Stilton cheese
2   Belgian endive, julienned
12 Belgian endive leaves, divided

SPICY WALNUTS

1   tablespoon butter
1/4 cup chopped walnuts
1   teaspoon cayenne pepper

WALNUT VINAIGRETTE

Kosher salt to taste
2   tablespoons sherry vinegar
3/4 cup walnut oil
1   shallot, finely diced
1   teaspoon chopped fresh thyme leaves
Freshly ground black pepper to taste

Prepare Spicy Walnuts; reserve. Prepare Walnut Vinaigrette; reserve. Toss greens with cheese, julienned endive and Walnut Vinaigrette in medium bowl. Arrange 3 endive leaves in fan shape on each of 4 plates. Mound mixed greens at base of fan and sprinkle Spicy Walnuts around edge of plate. Serves 4.

Spicy Walnuts

Preheat oven to 250 degrees. Melt butter in small ovenproof skillet; add walnuts and cayenne. Toss to combine; toast 15 minutes. Or toast in microwave: Melt butter in 1-cup glass measure; stir in walnuts and cayenne. Microwave on high 1 minute; stir and microwave in 30 seconds increments until lightly toasted. Makes 1/4 cup. Reserve.

Walnut Vinaigrette

Whisk salt with vinegar until dissolved in a medium bowl. Slowly whisk in oil until emulsified. Add shallot, thyme and pepper. Makes about 3/4 cup. Reserve.

🍎 Reduce walnuts to 1/2 tablespoon, vinaigrette to 1 tablespoon and cheese to 1/2 tablespoon per serving.

🍇 Benjamin Port (Australia); Sandeman Founder's Reserve Port (Portugal) — if served after the entrée.

SEARED SEA SCALLOPS *with Red Onion Marmalade*

Red Onion Marmalade (recipe follows)
1   tablespoon unsalted butter
12 large fresh sea scallops
2   tablespoons balsamic vinegar
1/4 cup chicken broth
Kosher salt and freshly ground black pepper to taste

Prepare Red Onion Marmalade; reserve. Heat butter in medium skillet; sear scallops. Add vinegar, broth, salt and pepper; cook over medium heat until thickened. Arrange Red Onion Marmalade on plate or over mashed potatoes; top with scallops. Reduce sauce in scallop pan until syrupy. Pour over all. Serves 4.

🍎 Sear scallops in skillet sprayed with a cooking spray. Use modified version of Red Onion Marmalade.

🍇 Rothbury Estate Chardonnay (Australia); Domaine Vocoret Chablis (France).

RED ONION MARMALADE

1	tablespoon grapeseed oil
2	medium-size red onions, sliced 1/8-inch thick
1/4	cup chicken broth
2	tablespoons whipping cream

Red Onion Marmalade

Heat oil in large skillet. Add onions and cook slowly until nearly caramelized, about 20 minutes, stirring occasionally. Stir in broth and cream; cook until liquid is reduced by half.

 Eliminate oil by cooking onions for marmalade in 1/4 cup broth. Substitute half-and-half for cream.

GRILLED ANGUS FILET MIGNON WITH MUSHROOM, DRIED CRANBERRY RAGOUT

4	(8-ounce) certified Angus filet mignon steaks
	Kosher salt and freshly ground black pepper to taste
3	tablespoons olive oil, divided
2	tablespoons unsalted butter
2	garlic cloves, minced
2	shallots, julienned
1	pound assorted cremini, shiitake and portobello mushrooms, cleaned and quartered
1/2	cup dried cranberries
1	tablespoon chopped fresh basil leaves
1	tablespoon chopped fresh thyme leaves
6	tablespoons veal stock (optional)
	Diced chives and Roma tomatoes for garnish

Season steaks with salt and pepper and rub with 1 tablespoon oil. Let stand at room temperature 15 minutes. Heat remaining 2 tablespoons oil and butter in medium skillet and sauté garlic and shallots over medium heat 10 minutes.

Add mushrooms and increase heat slightly. Sauté 15 minutes, or until mushrooms have softened and released moisture. Add cranberries, basil, thyme, salt and pepper. If desired, add stock and simmer 10 minutes. Or, continue to cook mushroom mixture on low while preparing steaks.

Grill steaks on barbecue about 10 minutes on each side for medium-rare or 15 minutes each side for medium. Divide mushroom mixture among 4 plates; top with a filet. Accompany with Scalloped Potatoes Riviera alongside meat. Garnish with chives and tomatoes. Serves 4.

Reduce beef filets to 6 ounces each. Eliminate oil and butter; sauté vegetables in 1/4 cup chicken broth. Serve with modified version of Scalloped Potatoes Riviera.

Estancia Pinot Noir; Monticello or Robert Mondavi Pinot Noir; any top quality red Burgundy from the Côte de Beaune (France).

SCALLOPED POTATOES RIVIERA

4   large russet potatoes, peeled and
    sliced 1/8-inch thick
4   cups milk
2   cups whipping cream
    Kosher salt, freshly ground
    black pepper and freshly grated
    nutmeg to taste
1 1/4   cups freshly grated Parmigiano-
        Reggiano cheese
6   tablespoons unsalted butter

Preheat oven to 350 degrees. Butter a 13x9x2-inch glass dish; set aside. Combine potatoes and milk in large saucepan; bring to a boil. Reduce heat and simmer 20 minutes, or until almost cooked. Transfer potatoes to prepared dish. Heat cream in separate pan; season with salt, pepper and nutmeg. Pour over potatoes until just barely covered. Dot with butter and sprinkle with Parmesan. Loosely cover dish with aluminum foil and bake about 10 minutes. Remove foil and bake until cheese is browned. Serves 8 to 10.

Substitute low-fat milk for whole and evaporated skim milk for cream. Reduce Parmesan to 1/2 cup and butter to 4 tablespoons.

CRÉME BRÛLÉE RIVIERA

4   cups whipping cream
1   cup milk
2   vanilla beans, split
1 1/4   cups sugar
12   egg yolks
1   teaspoon sugar for caramelizing
    Whipped cream, berries or
    sauce for garnish (optional)

Scald cream, milk and vanilla beans in large saucepan over medium-high heat. Combine sugar and egg yolks in medium bowl; beat until creamy. Slowly add hot cream mixture to sugar mixture, stirring with a spoon. After all liquid is incorporated, strain and chill immediately to stop eggs from cooking.

Preheat oven to 250 degrees. Divide mixture among 8 (1-cup) ramekins. Place ramekins in large pan and add water to come halfway up sides of ramekins. Bake 40 minutes, or until center of custard is set. Carefully remove ramekins from water bath, cool 20 minutes and refrigerate at least 2 hours.

Put ramekins on sheet pan, sprinkle sugar on top of each custard and place under broiler until sugar bubbles and caramelizes. Créme Brûlée can be made ahead and refrigerated. Serve garnished with whipped cream, berries or a sauce. Serves 8.

 Enjoy in moderation.

Dow Tawny Port (Portugal); Blandy's or Cossart Gordon Bual Maderia (Portugal).

FACING PAGE, FROM LEFT: *Shelly Drought, Redwood Grill; Polo Becerra, Post Oak Grill; Melissa Piper, Brennan's.*

FOLLOWING PAGE, FROM LEFT: *Joe Mannke, Rotisserie for Beef and Bird.*

MALLARD DUCK WITH BLACK WALNUTS
VENISON TENDERLOIN WITH BELL PEPPERS
UPSIDE-DOWN CARAMELIZED APPLE TART

Rotisserie for Beef and Bird is celebrating its 20th anniversary as one of Houston's premier restaurants. It has been recognized by top industry awards including the Ivy Award and Wine Spectator Grand Award for 10 consecutive years (one of only two Texas restaurants to be honored).

Owner Joe Mannke was one of the first Houston restaurateurs to develop regional cooking with local specialties such as wild game, duck, pheasant, quail, fresh herbs, fruits, vegetables and wines. He seeks out the best from many sources. The Wine Cellar holds more than 18,000 bottles from 850 labels.

Mannke has repeatedly proved himself a top chef — at Anthony's Pier 4 in Boston (the largest volume restaurant in the nation at the time) and at Disney World when it opened (he supervised more than 125,000 meals daily).

His life before he came to the United States in 1960 could be a movie. When he was six years old, he and his mother, sister and brother made a harrowing escape from Germany at the end of World War II and lived two years in a refugee camp until reunited with his father in Bavaria.

At 14, Mannke moved to Munich with the possessions he could carry on his bicycle. He apprenticed three years at a top German spa, then became a chef on a luxury train from Paris to Vienna. That led to hotel jobs in Africa, where he earned enough money to come to America. He arrived in New York in June 1960, on a Sunday and on Tuesday went to work at a job he found through a classified ad — it turned out to be at the famous Stork Club in New York.

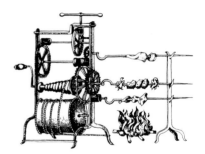

Rotisserie for Beef and Bird

His career took him to Bermuda, Puerto Rico, Boston, Florida and eventually Houston, where he was chef at the Hyatt Regency, which opened in 1974. His world experiences show up in some fashion on Rotisserie menus or in theme dinners that keep customers coming back time and time again. Mannke has elevated holidays to culinary art. Thanksgiving is a tour de force when staff members dress in costumes. Customers look forward to seasonal events such as Oktoberfest and the Texas Harvest Dinner with Texas wines.

He became an American citizen after five years in the U.S. and he takes particular pride in the Colonial architecture and paintings in the dining room depicting American scenes and heroes.

LITE FARE

Rotisserie for Beef and Bird specializes in fresh, seasonal foods produced from Texas' farms and wildlife. Wild game, game birds and fresh seafood are typically lean and can be grilled dry or with just a touch of olive oil upon request. Steamed vegetables and wild rice make great accompaniments to the grilled meats.

*Rotisserie for Beef
and Bird
2200 Wilcrest
Houston, Tx 77042
713-977-9524*

MALLARD DUCK WITH BLACK WALNUTS

4 mallard ducks, cleaned
1 cup buttermilk
2 garlic cloves, minced
2 tablespoons soy sauce
2 tablespoons honey
1/4 teaspoon ground ginger
6 juniper berries
2 bay leaves
1 cup peanut oil
1 cup all-purpose flour
1/4 cup unsalted butter
1 small white onion, chopped
12 large mushrooms, sliced
1/4 cup brandy
1 dozen ginger snaps, crushed
1 cup chicken broth, fresh or canned
1/4 cup port wine
1 cup whipping cream
 Salt and freshly ground black pepper to taste
1/2 cup toasted black walnut pieces

Use a sharp knife to cut along each side of duck breastbone and cut under breast to remove meat in one piece. Remove legs from carcass by cutting through the joint; discard any fat and skin. Place duck in large ceramic or glass bowl.

Combine buttermilk, garlic, soy sauce, honey, ginger, juniper berries and bay leaves; pour over duck. Cover and refrigerate overnight.

Remove duck from marinade and pat dry with paper towel. Heat oil in large skillet. Dip breasts in flour and sauté on both sides over medium heat until golden brown. Breasts should have a light pink color in the center. Remove from skillet, place on a heated platter and keep warm. Repeat procedure with remaining duck pieces.

Discard frying oil and heat butter in same skillet. Add onion and mushrooms; sauté a few minutes. Flambé by adding brandy and carefully lighting with a taper match. Add gingersnaps, broth and wine; bring to a boil. Stir with a wire whisk until gingersnaps are dissolved and sauce is thickened. Add cream; simmer for a few minutes but do not boil.

Strain sauce over ducks and garnish with walnuts. Accompany with wild rice and stewed apricots if desired. Serves 4.

 Reduce butter for sautéing to 2 tablespoons. Use low-sodium chicken broth. Substitute half-and-half for cream. The wild rice and stewed apricots will balance the fat calories. Recipe serves 8 adequately.

Nathanson Creek Merlot; Truchard Merlot; Duckhorn Merlot.

VENISON TENDERLOIN WITH BELL PEPPERS

12	(2-ounce) venison medallions, from back-strap if possible
4	egg whites, whipped
2	tablespoons lite soy sauce
1	tablespoon honey
2	garlic cloves, minced
2	tablespoons cornstarch
1/2	cup vegetable oil
1/2	cup unsalted butter
3	strips lean bacon, chopped
1/2	medium onion, diced
1/2	red bell pepper, diced
1/2	green bell pepper, diced
1/2	jalapeño pepper, seeded and minced
2	cups sliced portobello mushrooms
1	tablespoon all-purpose flour
1	teaspoon chili powder
1/2	teaspoon ground cumin
2	cups chicken broth, fresh or canned
1/2	cup red Zinfandel wine
1/4	cup cranberry jelly
2	bay leaves
4	juniper berries
1	cup whipping cream
	Salt and freshly ground black pepper to taste

Pound venison medallions with meat mallet to 2-inches by 1/4-inch thick; place in a ceramic dish. Mix egg whites, soy sauce, honey, garlic and cornstarch; spoon over venison, combine well and refrigerate covered 24 hours.

Heat oil in a heavy large skillet; add venison and cook over high heat on both sides until light brown, about 5 minutes. Do not overcook meat: it should be a little pink in the center. Add butter at the end to give the venison a delicious nutty taste. Remove venison from skillet, place on a heated platter and keep warm.

Reduce heat and add bacon to venison renderings in skillet; sauté. Add onion, bell peppers, jalapeño and mushrooms; sauté until glossy. Dust with flour, chili powder and cumin; combine well. Add broth, wine, jelly, bay leaves and juniper berries; bring to a boil. Reduce heat and simmer a few minutes until smooth. Add cream; heat but do not boil. Season with salt and pepper. Remove bay leaves and ladle over venison. Accompany with wild rice or any type of pasta. Serves 4.

Venison is a lean meat but this is a high-fat recipe. To cut fat calories, use only 1/4 cup canola oil and eliminate butter and bacon. Use low-sodium chicken broth. Substitute half-and-half for cream.

Chapoutier Côtes du Rhone (France); Llano Estacado Cabernet Sauvignon Cellar Select (Texas); Dunn Vineyards Cabernet Sauvignon (Napa or Howell Mountain).

UPSIDE-DOWN CARAMELIZED APPLE TART

1/2	cup water
1 1/4	cups sugar, divided
4	pounds Granny Smith apples
1	teaspoon cornstarch
1	teaspoon ground cinnamon
1/8	teaspoon ground cloves
1/2	cup unsalted butter
	Pastry Dough for a single crust pie (recipe follows)
	Fresh mint leaves and strawberries for garnish
	Whipped cream for garnish

Bring water to a boil in a heavy saucepan. Add 1 cup sugar and cook syrup to reduce until the sugar changes to a light brown color. Pour into a 9-inch baking dish; set aside.

Peel, core and quarter apples. Cut into lengthwise 1/8-inch slices; place in a large bowl. Combine remaining 1/4 cup sugar, cornstarch, cinnamon, cloves and butter in a small bowl. Toss with apples; place apples on top of caramelized sugar.

Preheat oven to 375 degrees. Prepare Pastry Dough. Roll dough to 1/4-inch thickness and place over apples, allowing edges to fall against the inside edge of dish. Use a fork to prick a few holes into dough to allow cooking steam to escape. Bake on middle shelf 1 hour.

Immediately invert tart onto a flat serving platter, garnish with fresh mint leaves and strawberries. Serve with chilled whipped cream. Makes 1 (9-inch) tart.

PASTRY DOUGH

3 3/4	cups cake flour, sifted
1/2	cup sugar
1 1/4	cups butter or margarine, at room temperature
1	egg
	Dash of vanilla extract

Pastry Dough

Place flour and sugar on pastry board; make a well. Put butter, egg and vanilla in center; knead quickly into a soft dough. Makes dough for 1 (9-inch) pie.

🍎 Enjoy this dessert in moderation. Recipe will serve 12.

🍇 Hogue Cellars Late Harvest Johannisberg Riesling (Washington); Ferrari Carano El Dorado Gold 1/2 bottle; Far Niente Dolce 1/2 bottle or Bernkasteler Doktor Beerenauslese (Germany).

ROASTED RED BELL PEPPER SOUP   SNAPPER ESCABECHE
CHARRED VEGETABLE PLATE
SHRIMP ARTURO (SCAMPI ARTURO)
CEVICHE SOLERO
MANGO MOUSSE

Solero was one of the first new-wave restaurants that are revitalizing the downtown area. It opened in April 1997 in the 116-year-old Brashear Building that backs the Rice Lofts (the former Rice Hotel). The tapas restaurant and bar was an immediate hit with office workers and the cool crowd. They like to socialize at lunch, wait out the rush hour with a glass of wine or pleasant drink and dinner or grab a bite before or after the theater.

Inventive chef Arturo Boada, a partner in the venture with Chuck Russell and Sharon Roeske Haynes, says tapas' time has come. These delectable bites of this and that, so popular in Spain, suit today's lifestyles. They appeal to those who are downsizing meals and often order a couple of appetizers instead of an entrée or ask for an appetizer portion of an entrée. Tapas bars are lively, convivial settings that encourage sharing.

Boada concentrates on popular Spanish tapas such as olives, fried calamari, Spanish anchovies, manchego cheese and Spanish-style potato tortillas (omelets). In keeping with today's eclectic cross-cultural mixtures, he might add South American or Asian seasonings, housemade chorizo, house-cured olives or provocative fresh fruit purees. More substantial menu items include a mixed grill of shrimp, chicken, chorizo and beef; chicken and pork tamales topped with sautéed shrimp; and paella. Pan-fried Snapper Cakes with Spicy Roasted Pepper Sauce, Mussels Solero, Roasted Red Bell Pepper Soup and Ceviche are signature dishes. Sunday brunch tempts the appetite with delicious egg dishes.

The Brashear Building was completely renovated in 1991. It was built in 1882 and named for Henry

Brashear, a judge of the District Criminal Court and former vice president of Texas National Bank. Brashear's brother Sam was mayor of Houston from 1898 to 1900. To preserve its natural look, the owners left the exposed brick walls in place. Wooden floors, ceiling fans, the back bar built on site and plants add to the period feeling.

Roeske Haynes, a metal artist, designed the mosaic tables, booth tables, wine rack, hanging light fixtures of tea-stained burlap, chandeliers and wall sconces.

Boada has been involved in many of Houston's favorite restaurants as a creative consultant. Recent projects include Sabroso, a casual South American restaurant in the Rice Village and a Chinese restaurant in his native Colombia.

LITE FARE

Tapas are small appetizer portions that are great for light eating. Look for tapas that are low fat such as shrimp and chicken kebabs, grilled marinated vegetables, ceviche, marinated mushrooms and grilled chicken strips. Good entrée selections are a charred vegetable plate and steamed clams. Food is made with fresh ingredients and prepared to order.

Solero
910 Prairie
Houston, Tx 77002
713-227-2665

ROASTED RED BELL PEPPER SOUP

1	tablespoon olive oil
1	pound roasted, peeled red bell peppers (Solero uses canned peppers)
1	tablespoon chopped garlic
1/4	cup finely diced yellow onion
1	bay leaf
1	teaspoon Creole seasoning
1	teaspoon ground cumin
1	teaspoon salt
1	teaspoon fresh lemon juice
1	teaspoon Worcestershire sauce
4	cups water
1	cup whipping cream
	Charred corn kernels (see Note)
	Julienned corn tortillas for garnish

Heat oil in stockpot. Add peppers, garlic and onion; cook until onion is translucent. Add bay leaf, Creole seasoning, cumin, salt, lemon juice and Worcestershire. Add water and bring to a boil. Remove bay leaf and process in batches in blender or food processor until smooth. Add cream and process again until smooth. Divide among 4 to 6 bowls, and garnish with corn and tortilla strips. Serves 4 to 6.

Note: To char corn kernels, place an ear of husked corn on grill over heat. When charred, cut kernels from cob.

Eliminate salt and substitute evaporated skim milk for cream.

KWV Steen (South Africa); Conde de Valdemar Blanco en Barrique (Spain).

SNAPPER ESCABECHE

4	(6-ounce) snapper fillets, grilled until done
1	cup thinly sliced Roma tomatoes
1	cup tomatillos, husked
1	teaspoon chopped jalapeños
4	teaspoons chopped cilantro leaves
4	teaspoons chopped basil
1	cup julienned red onion
1/4	teaspoon ground cumin
4	teaspoons white vinegar
1	tablespoon fresh lime juice
1/2	cup pomace olive oil

Cut snapper into bite-size pieces. Combine snapper, tomato, tomatillos, jalapeños, cilantro, basil, onion, cumin, vinegar, lime juice and oil in a glass bowl. Cover and let sit 45 minutes at room temperature. Serves 4.

Reduce oil to 2 tablespoons.

Fall Creek Sauvignon Blanc (Texas); Condes de Albarei Albarino (Spain); Didier Daguencau Pouilly-Fumé "Pur Sang" or "Silex" (France).

CHARRED VEGETABLE PLATE

1 pound yellow squash, sliced 1/8-inch thick
1 pound zucchini, sliced 1/8-inch thick
1 pound red onions, sliced 1/8-inch thick
1 pound carrots, sliced 1/8-inch thick
6 to 8 cloves garlic, finely chopped
2 cups fresh corn kernels
1 tablespoon pomace olive oil
1/2 pound tomatoes, cut in 1/4-inch dice
Salt and freshly ground black pepper
1/2 tablespoon chopped cilantro leaves
1/2 teaspoon chopped fresh basil
1/2 teaspoon chopped fresh oregano
1/2 teaspoon chopped fresh rosemary
1/2 teaspoon chopped fresh thyme

Toss yellow squash, zucchini, onion, carrot, garlic and corn in a bowl. Heat oil in a large cast iron skillet over high heat; sauté vegetables. Add tomato and season with salt and pepper. Continue to cook until black speckles appear and vegetables are al dente. Garnish with cilantro, basil, oregano, rosemary and thyme. Serve on a platter. Serves 8.

This is a great low-fat, low-sodium recipe. An excellent source of vitamin A.

Preston Cuvée de Fume (White); Alderbrook Pinot Noir (Red).

SHRIMP ARTURO (SCAMPI ARTURO)

4 tablespoons pomace olive oil
2 tablespoons chopped garlic
10 (21/25 count) shrimp, peeled and deveined
2 tablespoons cilantro pesto
1 cup whipping cream
1/2 cup dry white wine
Salt to taste and freshly ground black pepper
12 ounces cooked jalapeño fettuccine
1/2 cup freshly grated Parmesan cheese
Cilantro sprigs and finely diced red bell pepper for garnish (optional)

Heat oil in skillet. Sauté garlic and shrimp just until shrimp turns pink. Add pesto, cream, wine, salt and pepper. Reduce heat and cook until slightly reduced, by one-fourth. Toss with pasta. Sprinkle with Parmesan. Garnish with a sprig of cilantro and finely diced red bell pepper if desired. Serves 2.

Reduce oil to 1 tablespoon and substitute half-and-half for cream. This recipe is adequate for 4 servings.

Giannina Vernaccia (Italy); Puliccio Orvieto Classico Barberani (Italy); Michele Chiarlo Gavi or Valditerra Gavi (Italy).

CEVICHE SOLERO

1   pound shrimp, peeled and deveined
1   pound boneless, skinless snapper fillets
1   tablespoon olive oil
1   tablespoon fresh orange juice
1   tablespoon white vinegar
2   cups fresh lime juice
1   tablespoon chopped garlic
1   tablespoon chopped red onion
1/2 cup diced red bell pepper
1   jalapeño, with seeds, diced
    Pinch ground cumin
1   teaspoon salt
1   tablespoon chopped cilantro leaves
2   tablespoons passion fruit puree (see note)
    Endive, lettuce, bell pepper strips and lime slices for garnish

Cut shrimp and snapper into 1-inch pieces. Cook shrimp, in boiling water to cover, 1 minute. Discard liquid, cover and refrigerate until chilled. Combine snapper, oil, orange juice, vinegar, lime juice, garlic, onion, bell pepper, jalapeño, cumin, salt, cilantro and fruit puree in large bowl. Add shrimp; cover and marinate in refrigerator at least 6 hours.

Serve on endive or lettuce strips garnished with pepper strips and lime slices. Serves 8.

Note: Available in the freezer section of Fiesta Marts and Whole Foods Markets.

🍎 Great recipe — enjoy!

🍇 Chateau Ste. Michelle Riesling (Washington); Gruner Veltliner Nikolaihof Wachau (Austria).

MANGO MOUSSE

1 1/2 envelopes unflavored gelatin
1/2   cup cold water
1   cup whipping cream (chill cream, bowl and beaters well)
1/4   cup sugar
1   cup mango puree
    Sauce, such as raspberry, black-berry or mango
    Fresh berries (optional garnish)

In a small bowl, dissolve gelatin in water. In a separate bowl, beat cream, adding sugar gradually, until stiff. Fold gelatin and cream into mango. Pour into 6 (1/2-cup) individual molds, which have been sprayed with nonstick vegetable oil spray. Refrigerate at least 2 hours.

To serve, unmold onto dessert plates and serve with sauce and berries. Makes 6 servings.

🍎 Enjoy in moderation.

🍇 Quady Electra Orange Muscat 1/2 bottle; Domaine des Baumard Quarts de Chaume 1/2 bottle (France).

CHAMPAGNE BRIE SOUP EN CROUTE
HERB SEARED AXIS VENISON *and Pinot Noir Sauce*
BLACK TRUFFLE WHIPPED POTATOES
WHITE CHOCOLATE ICE CREAM CHARLOTTE

Through several reincarnations — from the Remington to the Ritz-Carlton to the Luxury Collection — the St. Regis has always been recognized for fine dining.

Executive chef Charles Dash honed his talent in several prestigious hotels, clubs and resorts in Texas. Dash began his restaurant career as a bus boy and dishwasher at JoJo's in San Antonio, but soon worked his way up to lead cook for the San Antonio area. He earned a degree in hotel and restaurant management and later worked at the Four Seasons and the St. Anthony Hotel in San Antonio. He has a passion for ice carving and once owned his own ice-carving company. This year he won the bronze medal at the 1998 World Ice Art Championship in Alaska. He also trained extensively in wedding cake design and sugar blowing.

Many of Dash's creations are rooted in simple, home foods, but he gives them a creative tweak, adding truffles to mashed potatoes and champagne and a puff pastry dome to brie soup. He seeks out specialty ingredients such as dry-aged beef from Chicago and free-range axis venison from Broken Arrow Ranch in Texas.

New menus emphasize classical French dishes and tableside cooking. Black truffles, chipotle sauces, free-range chicken, charred tomato relish, tuna pastrami, wasabi mayonnaise and housemade pizzas are other standouts. The Dining Room offers an ambitious menu of worldly specials beginning with breakfast with such items as Cinnamon Brioche Buttermilk French Toast and Pecan Wood Smoked Salmon with tomato, capers, cream cheese and toasted bagel. Entrées offer a taste of the Mediterranean, South America, the Caribbean and Pacific Rim.

The Bar and Grill appeals to diverse tastes and specializes in wild game. Entrées include a Trio of Chops — three types of venison with Blackberry Demi Sauce — and Cedar Plank Roasted Chilean Sea Bass with Wild Mushroom

THE ST. REGIS
Risotto, Pistachio Pesto and Lemongrass Nage.

Guests can enjoy afternoon tea in the Tea Room where fine teas are served in a tranquil living room setting with classic accompaniments of sandwiches and pastries.

Named one of the Top Hotels in America and the Number One Hotel in Houston on the Conde Nast Traveler Gold List, the hotel offers luxurious accommodations and two Club Level floors with 24-hour room service and concierge service. The hotel was named to Gourmet Magazine's 1998 America's Top Tables list.

LITE FARE

Special requests are encouraged at this restaurant and will be responded to by a chef. Customizing dishes to your specific needs, whether health or religious, are a specialty of the house. You can even make requests when making reservations. The menu is heart-healthy friendly and features lean game meats, seafood and pasta dishes.

*St. Regis
1919 Briar Oaks Lane
Houston, Tx 77027
713-840-7600*

CHAMPAGNE BRIE SOUP EN CROUTE

2 tablespoons butter
1/2 cup finely diced celery
1/2 cup finely diced yellow onion
1/2 cup finely diced carrot
2 cups chicken broth
4 cups whipping cream
6 ounces Brie, peeled
2 bunches fresh tarragon, leaves only, finely chopped
1 teaspoon Old Bay seasoning
1 cup diced cooked chicken
Salt and white pepper to taste
3/4 cup champagne
6 puff pastry shells
1 egg, beaten

Heat butter in large saucepan; sauté celery, onion and carrot until translucent. Add broth; bring to a boil. Add cream and Brie; bring to a boil again; reduce heat to a simmer. Add tarragon, Old Bay seasoning and chicken; simmer 5 minutes. Season with salt and pepper. Cool soup.

Preheat oven to 400 degrees. Fill each ovenproof soup bowl about three-fourths full. Top with 2 tablespoons champagne, or to taste. Cover each bowl with puff pastry shell; press around top edge to seal. Brush with beaten egg, arrange bowls on baking sheet and place on middle rack in oven. Bake until golden brown, about 10 to 15 minutes. Watch carefully. Serves 6.

🍎 Eliminate butter and sauté vegetables in chicken broth. Substitute evaporated skim milk for cream. Decrease Brie to 3 ounces. Use low-sodium, defatted chicken broth.

🍇 Domaine Ste. Michelle Sparkling Wine (Washington); Coudoulet de Beaucastle Perrin (France).

HERB SEARED AXIS VENISON *and Pinot Noir Sauce*

1 (2 1/2-pound) boneless axis loin or beef tenderloin, trimmed
Dijon mustard
1/2 cup combined chopped fresh herbs of choice (rosemary, thyme, parsley and oregano)
1/4 cup extra-virgin olive oil
3 cups Pinot Noir Sauce (recipe follows)

Slice loin into 12 medallions. Pound medallions with a meat mallet to 1-inch thick; lightly brush each with Dijon. Sprinkle herbs on both sides.

Heat oil in large nonstick skillet. Sauté medallions over high heat on both sides until nicely browned, 2 minutes per side. Remove from skillet; keep warm. Do not overcook; meat should still be pink in the center.

Prepare Pinot Noir Sauce. Pour a pool of sauce on each of 6 plates, arrange venison on top and accompany with Black Truffle Whipped Potatoes and baby vegetables of choice, such as carrots and asparagus tips. Serves 6.

 Eliminate 1/4 cup oil for sautéing and brown medallions in a non-stick pan sprayed with a vegetable spray.

🍇 Abbaye de Valmagne (France) or Chateau Los Boldos Cabernet Sauvignon (Chile); Bonny Doon Old Telegram.

PINOT NOIR SAUCE

- 1 tablespoon clarified butter
- 4 shallots, finely diced
- 1 rib celery, finely diced
- 1 medium carrot, finely diced
- 1 (750-ml) bottle Pinot Noir
- 2 sprigs thyme
- 1 teaspoon black peppercorns
- 2 Roma tomatoes, diced
- 1 quart demi-glace (see Special Helps section)
- 2 tablespoons blond roux or 1 tablespoon cornstarch dissolved in 2 tablespoons wine or water
  Salt and freshly ground black pepper to taste

Pinot Noir Sauce

Heat butter in same skillet used to sauté venison. Add shallots, celery and carrot; sauté briefly. Add Pinot Noir, thyme, peppercorns and tomatoes; cook over medium heat until reduced to 1 cup.

Add demi-glace and bring to a boil; reduce heat and simmer 10 minutes until sauce coats the back of spoon. If necessary, add roux to thicken. Season with salt and pepper. For a velvety texture, whisk a small amount of soft butter into sauce just before serving. Makes about 4 cups.

This is a fairly low-fat, low-sodium sauce. Enjoy in moderation.

BLACK TRUFFLE WHIPPED POTATOES

- 20 Yukon gold potatoes (about 4 pounds), peeled
- 2 cups milk, divided
- 1/2 cup soft unsalted butter, divided
  Salt and freshly ground black pepper to taste
- 1 black truffle, minced (see Notes)
- 1/2 teaspoon truffle oil

Preheat oven to 350 degrees. Dice potatoes and drop into bowl of cold water to prevent discoloration. Boil potatoes in salted water until soft. Drain and spread potatoes on baking sheet. Put in oven 5 to 10 minutes to dry out. Do not let them brown in oven.

Put potatoes through a ricer or process in food processor; place in large bowl. Blend in 1 cup milk and 1/4 cup butter. Season with salt and pepper. Check seasoning and add remaining 1/4 cup butter if needed. Add just enough of the remaining 1 cup milk so that potatoes aren't dry. They should be moist and buttery. Mix in truffle and truffle oil. Pipe potatoes onto plates with pastry bag fitted with a star tip. Serves 6.

Notes: For variation, add 1/4 teaspoon minced or roasted garlic to potatoes along with butter.

For truffle and truffle oil, substitute julienned portobello mushrooms and mushroom oil.

 Reduce butter to 1/4 cup.

WHITE CHOCOLATE ICE CREAM CHARLOTTE

3 ounces white chocolate (such as Callebaut), chopped
3 tablespoons light corn syrup
3 cups milk
1 cup whipping cream
1/3 cup sugar, divided
11 egg yolks
Ladyfingers (recipe follows)
12 ounces white chocolate
Fresh berries, créme anglaise or berry coulis for garnish

Combine chocolate, corn syrup, milk, cream and half the sugar. Bring to a boil. Whisk together egg yolks and remaining sugar in a medium bowl.

Temper egg yolks by adding one-fourth of boiled cream while whisking constantly. Whisk tempered yolks into hot cream mixture. Reduce heat to low and continue to stir with a wooden spoon until mixture thickens enough to coat the back of the spoon. Pour through a fine strainer and set aside in an ice bath to cool. Freeze mixture in ice cream freezer according to manufacturer's instructions.

Prepare Ladyfingers. To serve, melt chocolate and pour onto a baking sheet. Cut 2-inch diameter circles of chocolate. Stand a Ladyfinger on each plate using a round cookie cutter to hold together if necessary. Put a scoop of ice cream in each cylinder. Place chocolate lid on top of each cylinder and garnish with berries, créme anglaise or a berry coulis. Serves 6.

LADYFINGERS

2 cups sugar
16 eggs, divided
1 tablespoon orange flower water
3 cups sifted all-purpose flour

Ladyfingers

Beat sugar and egg yolks in electric mixer on medium speed until mixture has whitened slightly and falls off the beater in a ribbon. Add orange flower water. Fold in flour and mix. In clean bowl with clean beaters, beat egg whites until stiff. Fold into flour mixture.

Preheat oven to 400 degrees. Line baking sheets with parchment paper or Teflon liners. To shape Ladyfingers: Insert the paste into a pastry bag, fitted with a 1/2-inch plain round tip. Holding bag straight up, pipe flat strips onto baking sheet in 3-inch lengths, spacing 1/2-inch apart. Each Ladyfinger cylinder needs to be 5 inches wide. This requires 3 sets of 2 strips each: strips will bake together. Sprinkle with powdered sugar, shaking any excess off of pan. Brush a little water on top; bake until golden brown, about 10 to 15 minutes.

When done, let cool. Roll into 2-inch diameter cylinders. Use as directed above or freeze. Makes 6 cylinders.

 Enjoy in moderation. This can serve 12 adequately.

Mathilde Cassis de Saintomage 1/2 bottle (France); Lustau Pedro Ximinez Sherry (Spain).

CEDAR PLANKED SALMON WITH RASPBERRY CHIPOTLE SAUCE
SOUTHWESTERN PASTA PRIMAVERA
GRILLED SHRIMP WITH TOMATO JAM
HONEY CRIMSON GLAZED PORK TENDERLOIN WITH MIXED GREENS AND TOASTED PECANS
TEXAS PECAN CHOCOLATE BOURBON TORTE *with Bourbon Créme Anglaise*

W hen did it happen? At some point in the past few years, the typical city dweller developed a new attitude about the home kitchen. Remember when families planned meals a week at a time and shopped from long lists? Now, especially with the young career crowd, almost the opposite is true. Houstonians who work long hours, have family obligations and limited leisure time are looking for something to make cooking and shopping easier — or even someone else to do the work.

We now turn to specialty stores such as Rice Epicurean Market for all types of home meal replacements. Is this a pizza night? Chinese? Italian? Take your choice from an array of freshly prepared meals to make your time in the kitchen your own.

Catering has come on strong and people are enjoying entertaining in their own homes. The surprise is that a supermarket — even a high-profile gourmet market — would offer turnkey catering. But Rice Epicurean Market saw the trend and designed Epicurean Catering Company to provide full-service from food, wines and servers to flowers, linen, china and silver rental.

Director is Douglas Dick and catering manager is Luzia Turner. Corporate executive chef Tom Palmer oversees nine professional chefs, one in each market, plus as many as 70 more chefs and support staff. They can handle anything from a birthday party for six-year-olds to white-tie-and-tails wedding or bar or bat mitzvah.

Epicurean Catering Company can deliver a brisket and fixings for a barbecue, a holiday dinner, an elegant kosher dinner, desserts for an after-theater party, gift baskets for your clients or wines and cheeses for a wine-tasting party. Or they can deliver the food and finish preparations in your kitchen using your serving dishes.

The catering company draws on the resources and buying power of the nine unique neighborhood specialty grocery stores for foods and a wide selection of wines. Rice prides itself on stocking the newest and most exclusive foods. They include emu, wild game, gourmet coffees and teas, wide assortments of oils, sauces and imported specialties. Rice is the only supermarket in Houston with in-store shops for Mrs. See's candy and Honey Baked Ham.

Another special feature is the Cooking School at Rice Epicurean Market, 6425 San Felipe. Director Peg Lee with local and international chefs, food personalities and cookbook authors conducts regular classes. Call 713-954-2152 for information.

———————————— *LITE FARE* ————————————

Check out Rice Epicurean's Haute Healthy weekly in-store specials that are low in fat but full of flavor. Chef Tom Palmer honed his heart-healthy culinary skills as the chef at the former Chez Eddy, Methodist Hospital's renowned restaurant known for low-fat, tasty dishes. This is definitely the place to pick up a healthy meal.

Rice Epicurean Markets
Epicurean Catering
Company
713-662-7709

CEDAR PLANKED SALMON WITH RASPBERRY CHIPOTLE SAUCE

1   untreated cedar plank, about 14 inches (available at Rice Epicurean Markets)
    Cooking oil
1   (2 1/2-pound) side of salmon
1/4 cup extra-virgin olive oil
2   tablespoons raspberry vinegar
1   tablespoon fresh minced rosemary
    Salt and freshly ground black pepper to taste
1/2 cup roasted raspberry chipotle sauce (Fischer & Wieser recommended), divided
    Rosemary sprigs for garnish

Preheat oven to 350 degrees. Season board by rubbing cooking oil into it and placing in oven 10 to 15 minutes. Board will snap and pop but don't be alarmed.

Remove skin and pin bones from salmon. Combine oil, vinegar, rosemary, salt and pepper; rub over salmon. Marinate in refrigerator 1 hour.

Place board in oven to get hot, about 5 minutes. Place salmon on board and brush with 1/4 cup sauce. Bake 10 to 12 minutes, or until fish is more than 90 percent cooked. Remove and brush with remaining 1/4 cup sauce. Return to oven 1 minute. Serve on board garnished with sprigs of rosemary. Serves 8.

 Eliminate oil in marinade and increase raspberry vinegar to 1/4 cup.

Bonny Doon Vin Gris de Cigare; Rex Hill Pinot Noir (Oregon); Ponzi Pinot Noir Reserve (Oregon) or Zaca Mesa Pinot Noir Reserve.

SOUTHWESTERN PASTA PRIMAVERA

1   pound penne pasta
3   tablespoons extra-virgin olive oil
1   yellow bell pepper, finely diced
1   red bell pepper, finely diced
1/4 cup roasted, peeled, seeded and diced green chilies
1   jalapeño pepper, seeded and minced
1   medium zucchini, cut lengthwise and sliced 1/8-inch thick
1   tablespoon minced garlic
6   Roma tomatoes, peeled and coarsely chopped, including juice
1/4 cup corn kernels
2   tablespoons chopped cilantro
1   teaspoon ground cumin
3   tablespoons dry white wine
    Salt and freshly ground black pepper to taste
1/4 cup freshly grated imported Parmigiano-Reggiano cheese

Cook pasta until al dente; drain, set aside and keep warm. Heat oil in large skillet over medium heat. Add bell peppers, chilies, jalapeño, zucchini and garlic. Sauté 2 to 3 minutes, or until peppers soften. Add tomatoes with juice, corn, cilantro and cumin. Sauté 2 minutes. Add wine to deglaze pan. Season with salt and pepper.

Add sauce to pasta; toss well. Serve with Parmesan sprinkled on top. Serves 4.

 There are a lot of complex carbohydrates and antioxidants in this low-fat recipe. Enjoy!

Torre Roa Dolcetto d'Alba (Italy); Pio Cesare Docetto d'Alba (Italy).

GRILLED SHRIMP WITH TOMATO JAM

1	tablespoon unsalted butter
2	tablespoons finely grated fresh ginger
2	garlic cloves, minced
1/4	cup cider vinegar
1	cinnamon stick
1	(25-ounce) can imported peeled tomatoes, drained, seeded and coarsely chopped
1/4	cup brown sugar
1	teaspoon ground cumin
1/4	teaspoon cayenne pepper
1/8	teaspoon ground cloves
1/4	cup honey
	Salt and freshly ground black pepper to taste
1	pound (21/25 count) pound shrimp, peeled and deveined

Melt butter in saucepan. Add ginger and garlic; cook over moderately high heat, stirring until fragrant. Add vinegar and cinnamon stick; cook until reduced to a glaze, about 1 minute. Stir in tomatoes, sugar, cumin, cayenne and cloves. Reduce heat to low and cook, stirring occasionally, until liquid has evaporated, about 1 hour. Discard cinnamon.

Stir in honey and season with salt and pepper. Transfer mixture to food processor or blender; puree until smooth. Cool.

Put shrimp into medium bowl; coat with tomato jam mixture and let marinate at room temperature 30 minutes. Light grill or preheat broiler. Grill shrimp about 2 minutes per side, or until lightly charred on outside and opaque throughout. Serves 4.

 Savor this low-fat, low-sodium recipe.

 Mark West Gewürztraminer; Julien Meyer Gewürztraminer (Alsace).

HONEY CRIMSON GLAZED PORK TENDERLOIN WITH MIXED GREENS AND TOASTED PECANS

1	(1-pound) pork tenderloin
2	tablespoons extra-virgin olive oil
1	teaspoon minced garlic
	Salt and freshly ground black pepper to taste
1/4	cup Russian Mustard (Sable & Rosenfeld brand recommended)
1/4	cup Wild Cranberry Splash with Chambord (Sable & Rosenfeld recommended)
1	(6-ounce) sweet potato, peeled and cut into 1/4-inch sticks
2	cups mixed field greens
1/2	cup toasted pecan pieces
1	ounce ricotta salata cheese, grated
1/4	cup white balsamic vinegar (Alessi recommended)

Remove fat and silver skin from tenderloin. Combine oil, garlic, salt and pepper in a small bowl; rub into tenderloin. For Cranberry Mustard Glaze, mix mustard and Wild Cranberry Splash. Grill tenderloin; brush with half the glaze. Complete cooking on slow side of grill or in a 325-degree oven until medium-rare or medium doneness. Brush on remaining glaze; keep warm.

Sprinkle sweet potato slices with salt and pepper; grill until tender.

To assemble salad, arrange greens in center of each of 3 plates. Slice pork diagonally and fan out on plate. Place 3 to 4 pieces of sweet potato on greens, sprinkle with pecans and cheese. Drizzle vinegar over salad. Serves 3 as an entrée and more as a first course.

 Eliminate oil and rub pork with garlic and herbs. Reduce pecans to 3 tablespoons.

 Conde de Valdemar (Spain); Bodegas Weinert Malbec or Catena Malbec (Argentina); Ridge Lytton Springs.

TEXAS PECAN CHOCOLATE BOURBON TORTE
with *Bourbon Créme Anglaise*

1/4	teaspoon salt
1 1/4	cups all-purpose flour
1/2	cup solid all-vegetable shortening
3	eggs, lightly beaten, divided
3	tablespoons water
1/4	teaspoon vinegar
1 1/2	ounces unsweetened chocolate
3	tablespoons unsalted butter
3/4	cup dark corn syrup
1/2	cup packed dark brown sugar
3/4	teaspoon vanilla extract
1	tablespoon bourbon
1 1/4	cup chopped pecans
	Bourbon Créme Anglaise (recipe follows)

Mix salt and flour together; cut in shortening with pastry blender or two knives. Measure 1 tablespoon beaten egg into a small bowl. Add water and vinegar; stir. Add liquid to flour mixture; stir until mixture holds together.

Lightly flour work surface and roll out dough to fit a 10-inch by 3/4-inch fluted tart pan with removable bottom. Fit dough into pan.

Preheat oven to 325 degrees. Melt chocolate and butter together in heavy saucepan over medium heat. Stir corn syrup and sugar into remaining eggs. Add chocolate, butter, vanilla, bourbon and pecans; mix well. Pour into prepared shell. Bake about 40 minutes, or until set. Let cool a few minutes on counter. To serve with Bourbon Créme Anglaise, pour a pool of sauce on each plate, place torte serving in sauce and drizzle some over top. Or, serve with whipped cream and raspberries. Serves 8 to 10.

BOURBON CRÉME ANGLAISE

2	cups milk
1/2	cup unsalted butter
1/2	cup sugar
1	tablespoon cornstarch
2	tablespoons bourbon
1	teaspoon vanilla extract
3	egg yolks

Bourbon Créme Anglaise

Combine milk, butter and sugar in a medium stainless steel or other nonreactive saucepan. Cook over medium heat until hot, but do not let boil. Dissolve cornstarch in bourbon and vanilla; whisk into egg yolks. Whisk a small amount of hot milk mixture into eggs. Add egg mixture to saucepan; whisk until thickened. Remove from heat, cool slightly and refrigerate until needed. Serve warm or cold. Makes about 2 1/2 cups.

 Relish in moderation. Serves 12 adequately.

Kiona Late Harvest Muscat (Washington); Chambers Muscat 1/2 bottle (Australia).

FACING PAGE, FROM LEFT: *Thomas Palmer, Tracy Teft, Vladimirr Smirnov, Tim Semenuk, Robert Maccarone, Rice Epicurean Markets; Luzia Turner, Epicurean Catering Company*

FOLLOWING PAGE, FROM LEFT: *Jim Mills, Lance Fegen, The Houstonian.*

FRAN FAUNTLEROY

Fran Fauntleroy was inspired to begin her own company, Houston Gourmet Publishing, after writing and marketing two successful cookbooks, "Six Flew Over The Cuckoo's Kitchens" and "Cuckoo, Too," with six lifelong friends.

She has been responsible for seven Houston restaurant cookbooks and eight Houston Gourmet menu guides. She has published and sold more than 175,000 of these books in the past 20 years!

Her high energy and great interest in Houston's fine restaurants is the springboard that keeps her busy thinking of new ways to spotlight the ever-changing dining scene of which she is so proud. Houston has arrived!

Following the success of "Dallas Is Cooking!," a cookbook highlighting the restaurants for which that city has become famous, Fran then initiated "Houston Is Cooking" with Ann Criswell. They have now joined together to create "Houston Is Cooking At Home" after their success with "Houston Is Cooking The Best." This special gourmet collector's cookbook showcases the city's most popular restaurants and chefs who have successfully brought Houston recognition on a national level.

In addition to being a wife to John, she is mother of three grown children — Glenda, Shelley and Parker — mother-in-law of their special spouses Robby, Mitch and Lara — and grandmother to Ginny, Rob, Parker, Mitchell and Matthew Garrett . They are all the blessings of her life.

ANN STEINER

Ann Steiner is a syndicated microwave columnist who with her co-author, CiCi Williamson, created and published two microwave cookbooks — "Microwave Know-How" and "Micro Quick!". The duo also developed and appeared in a microwave cooking video and have written articles for several professional and popular publications.

Her varied interests in the culinary arena include: cookbook editing (this is her third "Houston Is Cooking" publication), recipe development and testing for major food companies, cooking seminars and teacher training. Ann also has served as a judge for the national Beef Cook-Off and Celebrity Microwave Cooking Contest.

She received a Master's Degree from Ohio State University and a Bachelor's Degree from Miami University (Ohio). In 1992, the Federation of Houston Professional Women selected Ann as one of their "Woman of Excellence" honorees. She is a member of the Houston Culinary Guild, Les Dames d'Escoffier and the International Association of Culinary Professionals.

Married to high-school sweetheart Bill, Ann is the mother of Cindy, Cathy and Jeff, mother-in-law of Steve Walker and Mike Knight and Nanna to Christa, Madelyn, Adam and Katie.

HEALTHY RECIPE MODIFICATIONS *by Linda McDonald, M.S., R.D., L.D.*

The secret to healthy eating is to enjoy foods that not only taste good but are good for you. No food or recipe is "good" or "bad." How an individual food or recipe fits into a total diet determines the health benefits. Understanding food and learning how to use basic principles of balance, variety and moderation is smart eating.

The LiteFare tips, recipe modifications and nutrition information are provided to help you make informed choices. Use the nutrient analysis chart to check the difference between the original recipe and the modified version. Then decide whether to use the suggested modifications based on your particular health needs and your eating plans for the rest of the day. Remember that balance, variety and moderation are the keys to eating healthy.

RECIPE MODIFICATIONS

Recipes are usually modified to change one or more of the ingredients so that the outcome is more beneficial. The four basic reasons for modifying recipes are:

- To reduce fat and cholesterol.
- To reduce sodium.
- To reduce sugar.
- To add fiber.

A recipe can be modified in four ways:

- Eliminate an ingredient.
- Change the amount of an ingredient.
- Substitute one ingredient for another.
- Change the cooking method.

TO REDUCE FAT & CHOLESTEROL:

Limit the portion of meat, fish or poultry to 3-4 ounces per serving. The current dietary recommendations are to eat no more than 6 ounces of lean meat, poultry or fish per day.

Choose lean cuts of meat and trim all visible fat before cooking. This includes removing the skin of poultry, which can be done before or after cooking. If you are using a moist cooking method (stewing, boiling or covered casserole), remove the skin before cooking. If using a dry cooking method (baking, broiling or grilling), leave the skin on during cooking to keep the product from drying out, but remove the skin before eating.

Marinate lean cuts of meat to tenderize them by breaking down muscle fiber. This is done by the acid part of the marinade — vinegar, wine, pineapple juice, etc. Oil is not necessary. Prick the meat all over with a fork to allow the marinade to penetrate thoroughly.

Plan a variety of proteins — animal and vegetable. Cycle red meat, poultry and fish with dried beans, peas and lentils.

Use non-fat or 1-percent dairy products. Replace whole milk cheese with cheese made from skim milk, such as part-skim milk mozzarella. Try some of the new low-fat cheeses.

Select sharp Cheddar and other strong tasting cheese. Place cheese on top to have the strongest influence on your taste buds.

Prepared meats and cheeses should have no more than 5 grams of fat per ounce. Check the labels or ask the grocer where you shop.

Use fewer egg yolks and whole eggs in cooking. Substitute two egg whites for each whole egg.

Prepare eggless pasta in place of egg pastas. Most dry pastas are eggless, and most fresh pastas use eggs, but check the ingredient lables.

Sauté with broth, wine or water instead of oils or butter.

Microwave vegetables in a covered dish with just a small amount of water, rather than sautéing in oil or butter.

Make stocks, soups, sauces and stews ahead of time. Chill, then remove all hardened fat from the top. If there is no time to do this, skim off as much fat as possible. Then add several ice cubes. The fat will congeal and cling to the ice cubes, which can be discarded.

If you can't make your own stocks, look for low-fat and low-sodium canned beef or chicken broth. Be sure to defat canned broth by chilling until fat hardens, then skim off.

Use nuts, seeds, olives, cheese, butter, margarine and oils in moderation.

Olive and canola oils are the best choices for cooking. Use olive oil for sautéing and in salad dressings; choose canola for baking. But remember that oils are still fats.

Low-fat cooking methods include broiling, baking, roasting, poaching and stir-frying. Utensils for low-fat cooking are non-stick cookware, vegetable cooking spray and steamers.

Try the following low-fat substitutions:

Cream— 1/3 cup non-fat dry milk in 1 cup skim milk or canned evaporated skim milk.

Sour Cream— Plain non-fat yogurt or a blend of 1 cup fat-free or 1% cottage cheese + 1 tablespoon lemon juice.

Mayonnaise — 1 cup plain non-fat yogurt and 1/2 cup light mayonnaise.

TO REDUCE SALT AND SODIUM:

Salt is an acquired taste. Your taste for salt will diminish as you gradually reduce the amount you use. You will begin to enjoy the taste of the food rather than the salt.

Eliminate or reduce salt in all recipes except yeast breads where salt is necessary to control the growth of the yeast. Even in yeast breads, salt can usually be reduced; one teaspoon per tablespoon of dry yeast.

Use salt-free or low-sodium canned products. Rinse canned products, such as beans, with water before using.

Salt is not necessary in the boiling water when cooking pastas, rice, or other grains.

Add salt last, after tasting the food. Use just enough salt to correct the food's flavor. Remove the salt shaker from the table.

Nothing else tastes exactly like salt, but other seasonings can enhance the flavor of foods and compensate for the salt you eliminate. Use the following seasonings to add zest to foods:

Lemon or Lime Juice — Use on salads and cooked vegetables. For more juice, microwave 30-60 seconds before juicing.

Citrus Zest — The thin outer layer of an orange, lemon or other citrus peel.

Adds flavor to baked goods, sauces and other dishes. Use a zester or grater.

Flavored Vinegars — Balsamic, tarragon, raspberry or wine.

Dried Onion Flakes, Onion or Garlic Powder, Garlic Cloves.

Condiments — Worcestershire sauce, hot pepper sauce, mustard, soy, etc. are relatively high in sodium, but if used sparingly, can enliven foods without overdoing the sodium. Use a low-sodium version when available.

Herbs — Fresh herbs have the best flavor, but if not available, substitute 1/2 to 1 teaspoon dried herb per tablespoon of fresh herb. Crush the dried herb to release the flavor.

Wines & Liqueurs — If cooked at or above boiling temperature, the alcohol evaporates, eliminating most of the alcohol and many of the calories while the flavor remains.

TO REDUCE SUGAR:

Sugar can be reduced by one-third to one-half in most recipes. In cookies, bars and cakes replace the sugar you have eliminated with non-fat dry milk.

Brown sugar or honey is sweeter than sugar and may be substituted for white sugar using considerably less. Nutritionally they are all the same, so there is no advantage to brown sugar or honey.

Flavor can be enhanced with spices (cinnamon, nutmeg or cloves) and extracts (vanilla, almond, orange or lemon). Doubling the amount of vanilla a recipe calls for will increase the sweetness without adding calories. Be

careful about increasing spices to boost flavor when sugar is decreased. Cloves and ginger can easily overpower the recipe. Safest spices to increase are cinnamon, nutmeg and allspice.

When reducing sugar in a recipe, substitute fruit juice for the liquid or add fruits such as raisins, dried apricots, dates, prunes or bananas. Frozen orange or apple juice concentrate can be added. One tablespoon concentrate equals 1/4 cup fresh juice.

TO ADD FIBER:

Use more whole grains (bulghur, brown rice, corn, barley and oatmeal), vegetables, dried beans, split peas and lentils.

Substitute whole-wheat flour for white flour whenever possible. It is heavier than white flour, so use less; 7/8 cup whole-wheat flour for one cup white flour. Experiment to find out what works best in recipe. Some recipes will turn out well with all whole-wheat flour, others are better when half whole-wheat and half white flour is used.

Add wheat bran, oat bran, oatmeal or farina to baked products, cereals, casseroles and soups. Start with one or two tablespoons and increase gradually. Substitute up to 1/2 cup oatmeal or oat bran for part of the flour in baked goods.

Use unpeeled potatoes whenever possible in soups, stews or for oven fries.

Use whole-grain pastas and brown or wild rice.

SPECIAL HELPS

Some terms and recipes from restaurant owners and professional chefs may be unfamiliar to home cooks. Here are several terms that you may see frequently.

Achiote — a yellow seasoning and color from the seeds of the annatto tree. Used in Central and South American, Indian, Mexican and Southwestern cooking.

Ancho chilies — dried poblano peppers; dark reddish brown, about 4 inches long.

Brown Sauce — Brown Sauce (Sauce Espagnole) - One of the foundation or "mother" sauces of French cooking; the base for many other sauces. Here is an easy recipe.

  2 tablespoons oil
  1 small onion, finely chopped
  1/2 carrot, grated
  1 tablespoon finely chopped fresh parsley
    Pinch of dried thyme
  1 bay leaf
  1 1/2 tablespoons all-purpose flour
  1 1/2 cups beef broth or bouillon (see Beef Stock recipe that follows, use canned or dissolve 1 teaspoon instant bouillon granules in 1 1/2 cups boiling water.)
    Salt and freshly ground black pepper to taste

Heat oil in large skillet. Add onion, carrot, parsley, thyme and bay leaf. Stir in flour and simmer slowly until browned, about 10 minutes. Whisk in broth, season to taste (don't over-salt) and simmer about 2 minutes. Strain. Makes about 1 1/2 cups.

Capers — the small green berry-like buds of the caper bush used as a condiment or to give piquant flavor to sauces. Usually available bottled or pickled in vinegar.

Charred corn — Husk corn, place on grill and cook until charred, but not burned. Remove kernels from cobs.

Chipotle — Dried, dark red smoked jalapenos.

Chocolate — To melt in the microwave: place chocolate in a glass dish and melt on medium (50-percent) power, about 1 1/2 to 2 minutes per square, stirring midway through. Chocolate may not look melted; test by stirring to smooth.

Clarified butter — Often used in delicate, fine dishes because it doesn't burn as easily as whole butter. Melt butter (preferably unsalted) over low heat until foam disappears from top and sediment and milk solids collect in bottom of pan. Pour off clear butter; discard sediment.

Concasse — crushed, seeded fruit or vegetables, especially tomatoes.

Confit — (**confee**) — cooked meat (usually duck or goose) preserved under a layer of fat.

Coulis — (**coulee**) — pureed mixtures of fruits or vegetables.

Cream — when chefs list cream as an ingredient, they usually mean heavy cream of at least 36 percent butterfat.

Whipping cream can be substituted for heavy cream if it is not available. When whipped, whipping cream doubles in volume. Most whipping cream now is ultra-pasteurized for longer shelf life. Better texture and optimum volume are achieved if the cream, bowl and beaters are thoroughly chilled before the cream is beaten. Some supermarkets stock heavy whipping cream.

If light cream is specified, look for cream labeled coffee cream or table cream.

Deglaze — Pour off all but a tablespoon or two of accumulated fat from sautéed food; add stock, water, wine or liquid called for in the recipe and simmer, scraping up browned bits from bottom of pan with a wooden spoon.

Demi-glace (DIM-ee-glahs) — A rich brown sauce based on basic espagnole (see Brown Sauce listing above). It is mixed with beef stock and sherry or Madeira and simmered slowly until reduced by half to a thick glaze. Often used as the base for other sauces and as a glaze added to the pan at the last minute.

End Hunger Network — Many of the hotels and restaurants in this book contribute unused or specially prepared food to the End Hunger Network, a worldwide alliance of private and volunteer organizations committed to ending hunger in the world. The Houston Chapter sponsors the Red Barrel program of food collection in hundreds of local supermarkets and the End Hunger Loop, which collects food from restaurants and food service institutions and distributes it to area missions and shelters. EHN also sponsors other programs including Hunters for the Hungry and educational activities. Call 713-963-0099 for information.

Herbs — Fresh are preferred if of good quality. The rule of thumb in substituting dried herbs is one teaspoon dried for three teaspoons fresh.

Nopales — fleshy pads of the cactus (nopal) that also produces prickly pears (cactus pears).

Olive oil — Extra-virgin olive oil is preferred by most chefs because it is the finest quality and has distinctive flavor. It is generally used for salad dressings or uncooked dishes and not for frying, as are lower grades of olive oil, because it has a low smoking point.

Less expensive grades such as superfine virgin, virgin, pure (now usually labeled olive oil) or pomace are better for everyday use. Store olive oil in a cool, dark place.

Pasta — Make your own or purchase from supermarkets or pasta shops. Fresh pasta is best with light, fresh tomato sauces or delicate cream sauces; dried pasta, with heartier, long-simmered meat and red sauces.

Fresh pasta takes only 3 to 5 minutes to cook; dried may take as long as 15 minutes. Pasta should always be cooked "al dente," which means firm to the tooth. It should lose its floury taste, but not be hard or mushy. Never rinse cooked pasta with cold water unless using it for salads or holding it to serve later. Rinse in cold water or hold in ice water until needed. Plunge strainer of pasta into hot water to revive it, then drain and serve. For best quality, hold pasta in cold water no longer than 30 minutes.

Roasted Garlic — Remove the papery outer skin, but leave heads of garlic whole. Slice off about 1/4-inch of top. Place in one layer in baking dish that has a cover; drizzle with olive oil or dot with butter. Cover pan and roast at 350 degrees until cloves are soft, about 45 minutes. Use in recipes or separate cloves and squeeze to extract garlic pulp. Discard skins. Spread garlic on bread rounds or toasted French bread or use in dressings. Four heads of garlic yield about 1/4 cup.

Alternatively, wrap each head of garlic in aluminum foil and bake at 350 degrees 1 hour. Let cool 10 minutes.

Roasted Peppers — To roast fresh peppers, rinse and dry, place on a baking sheet in a 350-degree oven 7 to 10 minutes (or broil 4 to 5 inches from heat 5 minutes on each side, until surface of peppers is blistered and somewhat blackened.) Drop into ice water and let sit for a few minutes until skins rub off easily. You can also place roasted peppers in a paper bag or plastic bag and let sit until skins rub off easily.

Handle jalapeños and other hot chilies with care as peppers and fumes can irritate skin and eyes. Wearing rubber gloves is recommended. Removing walls and seeds of peppers cuts the heat.

Roasted Tomatoes — Rub tomatoes with olive oil; place on baking sheet. Roast in 450-degree oven until charred. Remove from oven; let cool. Peel off skins. Or heat a heavy cast-iron skillet until very hot. Add tomatoes and cook, turning occasionally, until skins begin to blacken and blister, about 10 minutes. Let cool until they can be handled, then peel.

Reduce — Cook a mixture down slowly until reduced by half or the amount specified. In contemporary cooking, reductions are frequently used to concentrate flavors or thicken sauces instead of thickening with flour or other starches.

Roux — A mixture of flour and fat that is the thickening base for many sauces and soups, particularly gumbo. The usual method is to heat oil until it is at the smoking point, then to whisk in flour and stir constantly until mixture is a dark mahogany brown, almost black.

Roux requires close attention; it must be stirred or whisked almost constantly for 45 minutes to an hour or it will burn.

It is much easier in the microwave. The following method is from newspaper microwave columnists Ann Steiner and CiCi Williamson in their first book, "Microwave Know-How:"

Heat 1/2 cup each oil and flour in a 4-cup glass measure. Microwave on high (100-percent) power 6 to 7 minutes, stirring every minute after 4 minutes, until a deep brown roux is formed.

Salad Greens — Popular salad greens include gourmet baby lettuces, which are variously known as field salad (also corn salad, field greens, lamb's lettuce, field lettuce and mache), mesclun and spring mix. Mixes sold in markets often include arugula, radicchio, mizuna and tat soi (popular Japanese greens; tat soi is slightly peppery like watercress), baby oak leaf and red tip lettuces, frisée and watercress.

Stock — Stocks made on the premises are the rule in professional kitchens. If you use canned broth, buy a good quality product. Avoid salty broth, purchase low-sodium broth or reduce salt in the recipe.

When making stock at home, use a non-aluminum pan. For clear stock, skim foam and scum off top as it accumulates. Stir as little as possible to prevent clouding. Stock should simmer slowly, not boil. Strain and cool quickly (setting the pan of stock in a container or sink of cold water speeds the cooling process). Chill, then remove congealed fat from top. Refrigerate or freeze.

Beef or veal stock: Combine 2 to 4 pounds beef bones and meaty soup bones or veal bones and trimmings (brown half the meat) in a stockpot. Add 3 quarts cold water; 8 peppercorns; 1 each onion, carrot and celery rib, cut in pieces; 3 whole cloves; 1 bay leaf; 5 sprigs parsley; and other desired herbs such as dried thyme. Cover and bring to a boil over medium heat; skim off foam. Reduce heat and simmer 3 hours, skimming occasionally. Follow above basic directions. Makes about 2 1/2 quarts.

Chicken stock: Place 3 pounds bony chicken parts in a stockpot with 3 quarts cold water; a quartered onion stuck with 2 whole cloves; 2 each celery ribs and carrots; 10 peppercorns; 5 sprigs parsley; and 1 bay leaf. Cover and bring to a boil over medium heat; skim off foam. Reduce heat and simmer partially covered, 2 to 3 hours, skimming occasionally. Add salt to taste after about 1 hour. Follow above basic directions. Makes about 2 1/2 quarts.

Fish stock: Place 2 pounds fish bones, trimmings and head in a stockpot. Add 2 quarts cold water; 1 each thinly sliced onion and peeled carrot; 10 white peppercorns; a large bay leaf; a sprig of thyme; 10 parsley sprigs; and 1 teaspoon salt. Cover and bring to a boil over medium heat; skim off foam. Reduce heat and simmer about 1 hour, skimming occasionally. Follow above basic directions. Makes about 1 3/4 quarts.

Shrimp stock: Place shells from 1/2 pound shrimp in saucepan with water to cover. If desired add a little salt, parsley, crumbled dried thyme and a bay leaf (or make a bouquet garni of herbs tied in a cheesecloth bag). Cover and bring to a boil over medium heat; skim off foam. Reduce heat and simmer 10 to 15 minutes. Follow above basic directions. Makes about 1 quart.

Sweat — Place chopped vegetables or other ingredients in a partially covered pan over low heat and heat until moisture beads form and vegetables are softened.

Vinegar — Use clear white vinegar unless recipe specifies another type such as cider, fruit-flavored, rice wine or balsamic vinegar (dark, aged Italian vinegar).

Zest — The thinnest colored part of the peel only (no pith or white membrane); usually refers to citrus fruit.

SHOPPING GUIDE

Houston abounds in sources for ethnic and special ingredients called for in recipes in "Houston Is Cooking at Home." Specialty supermarkets are stocked with exotic produce, fresh herbs, special sauces, condiments, spices, flavored oils and vinegars, juices, pastas, breads, pastries, frozen patty shells and filo dough, canned imported items as well as a wide variety of coffees and teas.

Ethnic markets run the gamut from Mexican to Middle Eastern, Caribbean, Chinese, Japanese, Korean, Vietnamese, Thai and Indian. Visiting these markets makes for interesting weekend excursions.

Bakeries such as **French Gourmet** (two locations) sell ready-made puff pastry dough in addition to specialty breads, cakes and other pastries.

Houston is fortunate to have a number of fine bread bakeries including **Empire Baking Company**, 1616 Post Oak Blvd.; **French Riviera Bakery & Cafe**, 3032 Chimney Rock; **Great Harvest Bread Company** (two locations); **la Madeleine** (several locations); **La Victoria**, 7138 Lawndale; **Moeller's Bakery**, 4201 Bellaire Blvd.; **Patisserie Descours**, 1330-D Wirt Road; **Stone Mill Bakers** (two locations); **Three Brothers Bakery** (three locations); and **Whole Foods Markets** (three locations).

GENERAL

Auchan, 8800 W. Sam Houston Parkway, between Beechnut and Bissonnet (281-530-9855). A hypermarket stocked with a United Nations of imported foods from around the world including hundreds of cheeses, international wines, spices, fresh produce, meats, seafood and fish, a full range of grocery items and baked goods from the in-store bakery.

Fiesta Marts, more than 40 locations. Excellent source for fresh produce and foodstuffs from the world's markets — baked goods, ethnic foods, specialty foods, meats and seafood, cooking utensils, condiments, spices, wide selection of Mexican cheeses, prepared take-out foods and wines. Stores vary in size and character with the neighborhoods they serve. Some have coffee and tea bars, in-store delicatessens and sushi bars. Fiesta at 1005 Blalock Dr. off I-10 (the Katy Freeway) offers regularly scheduled cooking classes. Call 713-869-5060, extension 299.

Kroger Signature stores (27 locations throughout the city) are special-concept stores with a wide variety of specialty and gourmet foods and wines. At the Signature Store, 3665 Highway 6 at Settler's Way in Sugar Land (281-980-8888), a wine steward is in charge of what Kroger boasts is the largest selection of wines in a Texas supermarket. The produce department offers more than 450 varieties including imported, ethnic and organic items, prepared salads, bagged vegetables and a juice bar.

Signature stores are upscale markets showcasing in-store delicatessens, bakeries and salad bars; specialty foods; fresh meats and seafood; prepared take-out items; and floral shops. Some do catering.

Randalls Flagship stores (six locations with two more remodeled stores opening soon at Westheimer/Gessner and Bellaire/Rice). Top-drawer supermarkets known for fresh meats, fish and seafood, produce, domestic and imported specialty foods. Flagship stores have in-store bakeries with a pastry chef; specialty breads; delicatessens; coffee-tea bars; expanded wine departments; fresh salad bars; take-out specialties including an assortment of hand-made pizzas, sandwiches, salads and rotisserie chicken; and floral shops. They offer Busy Chef by Randalls home meal replacements and catering and can do party trays, corporate luncheons and events from 10 to 500. High-quality packaged meals featuring good-as or better-than-homemade specialties are a holiday tradition.

Rice Epicurean Markets / Epicurean Catering Company, nine locations - see page 119.

Whole Foods Markets (three locations) showcase natural foods: organically grown fruits and vegetable, imported and domestic sauces, condiments, bulk grains, cereals, herbs, spices and seasonings, cheeses, dairy products including yogurts and ice creams, frozen foods, additive-free meats and chicken, specialty breads and other baked goods, wines, beers, teas, coffees, health foods, local and regional products including preserves, sauces and cookies.

Stores feature Whole Foods' own brand-name breads, jarred sauces, in-house bakeries, juice bars and delis with an international mix of natural pasta and rice dishes, sandwiches, salads, hot entrees and side dishes. Catering available.

SPECIALTY SHOPS

Ferrari Fresh Pasta (three locations) offer an excellent assortment of fresh and custom-made pastas, sauces, condiments, flavored oils and vinegars, breads and baked goods, take-out specialties, decorative serving utensils and accessories as well as full-service catering.

Leibman's Wine & Fine Foods, 14010-A Memorial Dr. at Kirkwood (281-493-3663). Ettienne Leibman hand-picks an extensive collection of wines, hard-to-find spices, oils, vinegars, mustards and other condiments, imported pastas, candies including Godiva chocolates and sugar-free varieties, specialty meats and one of the city's best selections of cheeses. In-store deli provides exceptional Chicken Salad Afrique, sandwiches, pasta and rice salads, scones and incomparable English bread pudding, a house specialty. Catering available for kosher holidays, luncheons and corporate and special events. Excellent source for custom gourmet gift baskets.

Richard's Liquors and Fine Wines (several locations). Established in 1949, Richard's has done much to educate Houston's palate for fine wines. Larger stores feature wines from around the world including great vintages and large selections of French Bordeaux and Burgundies, specialty Cognacs, brandies, fruit brandies and Scotches, imported and domestic cheeses and caviars. Custom gift baskets are a specialty.

Spec's Liquor Warehouse & a Whole Lot More Store, 2410 Smith St. (713-526-8787). Spec's is a 28,000-square-foot facility packed with one of the city's most impressive collection of wines, liquors, liqueurs and specialty foods. They include pâtes; domestic and imported cheeses (more than 300); spices and seasonings; oils and vinegars; salsas; sauces; pastas (more than 300); coffees (more than 90, most roasted in-house) and teas; preserves; chocolates and other candies; specialty meats and condiments. In-house delicatessen features made-to-order sandwiches, soups and salads.

Family-owned and operated, Spec's is known for wide selections of wine and specialty foods at good-value prices and for custom-designed gourmet gift baskets.

Yapa Kitchen and Fresh Take Away, 3173 Holcombe Blvd. (713-664-9272). High-quality prepared foods include fresh pasta, sauces, imported oils, vinegars, cheese, gourmet foods and desserts from Marilyn Descours' Patisserie Descours. Limited catering available.

MISCELLANEOUS

Cost Plus World Markets (four locations). Stores offer imported specialty foods — pastas, bread mixes, rice, dried beans, sauces, spices, seasonings, condiments, coffees and teas from all over the world — as well as housewares; linens, pottery, flatware and crystal; decorative objects; furniture; and clothes. Beans can be ground to order for more than 60 coffees and more than 40 teas are stocked.

Kitchen & Company (three locations and a fourth store opening in Sugar Land later this year). The kitchen, dining and entertaining superstores offer more than 23,000 items ranging from name brand cookware and bakeware to china, crystal, gourmet foods, decorative accessories and cookbooks. Among specialty foods are sauces, salsas, condiments, pastas, coffees, teas and snack items. Stores also sponsor cooking classes, special events and project demonstrations. Toll-free telephone number is (800-747-7224). Address for shopping via the Internet is: http://www.kitchenandcompany.com

Williams-Sonoma (three locations) — features everything to outfit the gourmet kitchen from fine-quality cooking utensils and small appliances to table linens and specialty food items. Their forte is gourmet oils and vinegars; pasta; grains; salsas and sauces; china, pottery and table accessories; coffee grinders and coffee makers; spices; cookbooks; gadgets and housewares. Cooking demos and classes offered regularly.

INTERNATIONAL MARKETS

Asian
There are several markets in Chinatown east of Main Street around McKinney and St. Emanuel and another cluster outside Loop 610 on and around Bellaire Boulevard.

Asiatic Import Company, 909 Chartres (713-227-7979). Family-owned; offers bottled sauces, canned goods, condiments, spices and seasonings, wine, teas as well as cooking utensils and gift items.

Daido Market, 11138 Westheimer (713-785-0815). Japanese market with mostly basic seasonings and sauces, canned goods and limited fresh produce, seafood and tuna.

Diho Market, 9280 Bellaire Blvd. (713-988-1881). Extensive stock of Chinese and Asian products, fresh meats, fish, wines, sauces, frozen and prepared items, fresh produce and standard sauces and condiments.

Dynasty Supermarket in Dynasty Plaza, 9600 Bellaire Blvd. (713-995-4088). Full-line supermarket of Asian and Chinese staples, condiments and hot deli items, meats, fresh fish and seafood, wines and beers.

Hong Kong Food Market, 5708 S. Gessner Dr., (713-995-1393); 10923 Scarsdale (281-484-6100) and 13400 Veterans Memorial Dr. (281-537-5280). Full-service supermarkets with wide range of fresh Asian produce; exotic fruits, juices and vegetables, such as Chinese water spinach; fresh meats, chicken and fish; fresh lobster and other seafood; sauces; baked goods; tofu; noodles and rice; spices, seasonings and condiments; fresh bamboo leaves.

Kazy's Gourmet, 11346 Westheimer (281-293-9612), offers Japanese and other Asian ingredients and specialties.

Kim Hung Supermarket, 1005 St. Emanuel (713-224-6026) and 12320 Bellaire Blvd. (281-568-3040). Full-service markets specializing in Chinese and Asian imported foods, fresh produce, fresh seafood, sauces, condiments and noodles.

Long Sing Supermarket, 2017 Walker (713-228-2017). Small-scale supermarket with hot deli; fresh produce, meats, fish and seafood; frozen prepared items; condiments, sauces, seasonings, noodles and tofu.

Viet Hoa Supermarket, 10828 Beechnut (281-561-8706). Complete supermarket with fish market, produce shop and wide assortment of Asian ingredients including Chinese, Vietnamese and Thai specialties.

Vientiane Market, 6929 Long Point (713-681-0751). Small but well-stocked market specializing in Thai and Vietnamese foods, some Chinese.

Selection of fresh produce; meats and fish; canned goods, traditional sauces, spices, seasonings such as tamarind and yanang leaves, pickles, pickled limes and mixes; cassia flowers, noodles, spring roll skins, coconut milk, palm sugar, curry pastes, fish powder and chilies.

Welcome Food Center, Inc., 9180 Bellaire Blvd. (713-774-8320). Supermarket featuring fresh meats, fish and seafood, fresh produce, staples of Asian cooking.

Middle Eastern, Persian

Abdallah's, 3939 Hillcroft (713-952-4747) is a restaurant providing Middle Eastern dishes such as hummus, tabbouleh and vegetables; stocks a boutique assortment of Middle Eastern spices, herbs, breads, canned goods and prepared desserts. Take-out available.

Antone's Import Co. (several locations). Specializes in spices, sauces, Middle Eastern and other imported foods and wines along with world-class poor boys.

Droubi's Imports and restaurants — several locations including Droubi's Bakery & Delicatessen, 7333 Hillcroft (713-988-5897); and 3163 Highway 6 South in Sugar Land (281-494-2800). Middle Eastern, European imports and other specialty foods from around the world including kosher foods from Israel. Known for Middle Eastern breads, hummus, falafel, tabbouleh, shish kebab and deli classics. Take-out and full catering available.

Phoenicia Specialty Foods, 12126 Westheimer (281-558-8225). Middle Eastern and Mediterranean grains, rice, beans, sauces, spices, pastries, meats, cheeses and other gourmet foods at top-value prices. Many available in bulk. Phoenicia Deli, which offers some products and take-out Middle Eastern specialties, such as tabbouleh and falafel, is nearby.

Super Sahel, 5627 Hillcroft (713-266-7360). Small shop with necessities for Persian cooking such as basmati rice, couscous, pickled garlic, ghormeh sabji herb mix, barberries, canned okra, sumac and other traditional spices, sesame candy; pomegranate and other exotic syrups and preserves, chutneys.

Super Vanak International Food Market & Deli, 5692 Hillcroft (713-952-7676). Stocks all the staples of Persian and other Middle Eastern cuisines — sour cherry and pineapple syrups, mint water, barberries, fig jam, quince preserves, teas and coffee, pickles, sumac and spice mixes, pickled lemons, camomile flowers; curry paste, chutneys, fesenjoon (a mixture of walnuts, tomato paste, mushrooms, pomegranate paste and juice, onion and canola oil); taftoon bread, basmati rice, tahini, dried fruits.

Indian

India Grocers, 6606 Southwest Freeway at Hillcroft (713-266-7717) and 5604 Hillcroft (713-782-8500) are stocked with classic spices and foods from India, Pakistan and around the world. Wide variety of rices, dal (lentils), spices, gram flour (besan), pickles, chutneys and other condiments, ghee (clarified, reduced butter), pistachios, peanuts, cashews, almonds and other nuts, tahini and other pastes, mixes, fresh produce including popular Indian vegetables and mangos, breads, desserts, frozen and canned foods at good-value prices.

Patel Brothers, 5815 Hillcroft (713-784-8332). Stocks all the accoutrements of Indian cooking from almond oil and fresh curry leaves to exotic ice creams. Good source for saffron and other spice, raisins and figs, cashews, pistachios and other nuts, ginger and garlic pastes, dal (lentils), a wide variety of chutneys, tamarind and fresh fruit, especially mangos in season.

RECIPE NUTRITIONAL ANALYSIS

The information listed below was calculated by computer nutrient analysis of each recipe and the recipe prepared according to the modification tip (*Modified Recipe). Because the nutrient content of food varies depending on growing conditions, season, transit time to market and other factors, the numbers given should be considered estimated values.

The nutrient analysis is for one serving. If a range of servings is given (serves 6 to 8), the first number was used for the analysis. If you serve more or less than the suggested serving, adjust the nutrient numbers accordingly.

The nutritional analysis of each recipe includes all the ingredients that are listed in that recipe, except for ingredients for which no amount is given, for instance "salt to taste" or ingredients labeled as "optional." If an ingredient is presented with an option ("1 cup chicken or vegetable broth" or "2 to 4 tablespoons") the first item or number listed was used in the nutritional analysis.

* *Recipes modified according to the instructions at the end of the regular recipe designated with an apple. Regular recipes with an asterisk are considered healthy.*

	Portion	Calories	Protein (g)	Carbohydrate (g)	Fat (g)	% Fat Calories	Cholesterol (mg)	Sodium (mg)	Dietary Fiber (g)
*Alice's Chicken Delight (Nit Noi)	1 serving	611	26	95	15	22	101	686	10
*Modified Recipe	1 serving	611	26	95	15	22	101	563	10
Baked Alaska (Post Oak)	1 serving	960	15	122	49	45	240	474	2
*Modified Recipe	1 serving	911	16	126	41	40	204	470	2
Beef Debris Gumbo (Brennan's)	1 serving	413	42	14	20	45	120	1555	3
*Modified Recipe	1 serving	256	24	14	11	40	54	289	3
Beer Cheese Soup (Redwood)	1 serving	653	17	11	60	81	190	684	1
*Modified Recipe	1 serving	255	23	20	8	27	17	193	1
Black Truffle Whipped Potatoes (St. Regis)	1 serving	419	8	57	19	39	52	55	4
*Modified Recipe	1 serving	352	7	57	11	28	32	54	4
Braised Beef with Brown Sauce (Ambassador)	1 serving	292	29	7	15	48	86	2536	2
*Modified Recipe	1 serving	289	34	11	11	36	73	1561	2
Bread Soup (Aldo's)	1 serving	553	19	57	28	46	23	1867	2
*Modified Recipe	1 serving	440	21	57	16	31	23	338	2
Cabbage Soup (Nit Noi)	1 serving	342	36	17	16	40	54	1080	3
*Modified Recipe	1 serving	262	28	16	11	36	54	443	3
Cedar Planked Salmon with Sauce (Rice)	1 serving	268	29	1	16	55	80	105	0
*Modified Recipe	1 serving	209	29	1	9	41	80	105	0
Ceviche (Café Noche)	1 serving	344	24	22	19	48	109	630	3
*Modified Recipe	1 serving	225	24	20	7	27	86	332	2
*Ceviche (Solero)	1 serving	146	23	7	3	20	94	401	1
Champagne Brie Soup en Croute (St. Regis)	1 serving	889	21	17	82	82	308	781	1
*Modified Recipe	1 serving	388	27	32	16	37	74	565	1

	Portion	Calories	Protein (g)	Carbohydrate (g)	Fat (g)	% Fat Calories	Cholesterol (mg)	Sodium (mg)	Dietary Fiber (g)
*Charred Vegetable Plate (Solero)	1 serving	159	4	33	3	16	0	167	5
*Chicken Griselda (La Tour)	1 serving	470	53	33	12	23	125	699	3
*Modified Recipe	1 serving	470	53	33	12	23	125	193	3
Chicken Grogorio (Cavatore)	1 serving	778	49	18	56	65	256	317	2
*Modified Recipe	1 serving	449	43	18	22	44	142	139	2
Chicken with Dry Red Peppers (Ambassador)	1 serving	230	25	15	7	29	63	1027	2
*Modified Recipe	1 serving	230	25	15	7	29	63	461	2
Chilled Jumbo Shrimp with Remoulade (Redwood)	1 serving	218	8	3	20	81	81	216	0
*Modified Recipe	1 serving	110	7	2	8	67	61	234	0
Chocolate Molten Souffle with Sauce (Brennan's)	1 serving	816	12	90	47	51	263	237	2
Corn Crusted Redfish with Sauce (Post Oak)	1 serving	895	51	34	64	63	316	654	6
*Modified Recipe	1 serving	463	47	29	18	35	182	245	3
Corn Risotto (Mark's)	1 serving	233	7	26	13	46	26	452	3
*Modified Recipe	1 serving	174	6	26	7	33	13	114	3
Cornmeal Drop Biscuits (Brennan's)	1 serving	186	5	22	8	41	24	257	1
Crème Brulee (Riviera)	1 serving	666	8	43	53	70	486	71	0
Crispy Chicken with Ginger & Sauce (Empress)	1 serving	356	39	22	10	27	99	1933	0
*Modified Recipe	1 serving	356	39	22	10	27	99	104	0
Crispy Red Snapper (Nit Noi)	1 serving	451	44	33	15	29	128	2011	5
*Modified Recipe	1 serving	451	44	33	15	29	128	701	5
Dominic's Penn Pasta (Damian's)	1 serving	532	34	30	30	52	139	375	3
*Modified Recipe	1 serving	348	27	32	13	33	69	136	3
Eggplant Scechuan Style (Ambassador)	1 serving	100	3	18	3	21	0	935	7
*Modified Recipe	1 serving	100	3	18	3	21	0	288	7
Fettuccine Roma (Cavatore)	1 serving	1040	42	94	55	48	249	581	4
*Modified Recipe	1 serving	764	39	94	25	30	146	431	4
Field Greens & Artichoke Salad (Arcodoro)	1 serving	481	11	14	45	80	5	728	4
*Modified Recipe	1 serving	149	5	8	12	67	2	230	3
Filet Mignon (Empress)	1 serving	806	37	17	68	74	88	1079	7
*Modified Recipe	1 serving	389	37	17	20	46	88	436	7
Fillet of Snapper with Sauce (Aldo's)	8-oz fillet	402	33	7	25	56	84	170	0
*Modified Recipe	6-oz fillet	270	26	8	13	46	55	153	0
Fried Calamari (Cavatore)	1 serving	608	31	18	45	66	370	339	1
*Modified Recipe	1 serving	245	22	16	9	33	196	312	1
Goat Cheese Salad with Vinaigrette (Grille 5115)	1 serving	566	16	20	49	75	45	527	3
*Modified Recipe	1 serving	293	9	12	24	72	22	360	2
Gougeres (DeVille)	1 Gougeres	59	3	3	4	58	39	111	0
Green Enchiladas (Café Noche)	3 enchiladas	1179	64	78	73	54	156	657	12
*Modified Recipe	1 enchilada	259	17	23	12	40	40	142	4
Grilled Corn Chowder with Potatoes & Thyme (Mark's)	1 serving	679	22	33	53	68	190	1541	4
*Modified Recipe	1 serving	307	22	44	7	19	24	701	4

	Portion	Calories	Protein (g)	Carbohydrate (g)	Fat (g)	% Fat Calories	Cholesterol (mg)	Sodium (mg)	Dietary Fiber (g)
Grilled Filet Mignon with Ragout (Riviera)	8-oz filet	602	51	25	33	49	157	118	4
*Modified Recipe	6-oz filet	454	49	25	22	44	121	92	4
Grilled Pork Chops with Sauce (Bistro Lancaster)	1 serving	335	28	4	22	60	72	463	1
*Modified Recipe	1 serving	197	21	4	10	46	57	61	1
*Grilled Shrimp with Tomato Jam (Rice)	1 serving	261	19	39	4	14	169	211	2
Herb Seared Venison with Sauce (St. Regis)	1 serving	504	45	10	28	50	125	895	1
*Modified Recipe	1 serving	425	45	10	19	40	125	895	1
Honey Pork Tenderloin with Greens & Pecans (Rice)	1 serving	497	37	21	30	54	94	351	3
*Modified Recipe	1 serving	335	36	19	13	35	94	351	3
Jalapeno BBQ Shrimp/Pico de Gallo Rice (Houstonian)	1 serving	432	14	69	11	22	78	1885	4
*Modified Recipe	1 serving	251	11	32	9	31	79	153	2
*Jalapeno Corn Muffins (Redwood)	1 serving	130	4	23	2	17	24	250	1
Lamb Enchiladas (Post Oak)	1 serving	814	53	47	46	51	194	1851	4
*Modified Recipe	1 serving	577	43	40	28	43	134	492	4
Lamb Shanks Osso Buco Style (Aldo's)	1 serving	860	53	33	52	54	164	167	5
*Modified Recipe	1 serving	671	53	33	31	42	164	167	5
Lemon Baked Cheesecake (Empress)	1 serving	602	10	42	45	66	203	393	1
*Lentil Soup (La Tour)	1 serving	239	19	32	4	16	0	780	14
*Modified Recipe	1 serving	239	19	32	4	16	0	106	14
Pork Loin with Perfumes (Arcodoro)	1/6 recipe	638	51	48	25	36	134	424	5
*Modified Recipe	1/8 recipe	464	38	36	17	33	101	318	4
Macadamia Nut Chocolate Caramel Torte (Houstonian)	1 serving	785	7	94	47	51	116	235	3
Mallard Duck with Walnuts (Rotisserie)	1/4 recipe	1343	70	39	99	66	327	715	2
*Modified Recipe	1/8 recipe	576	34	20	39	61	127	175	1
Mango Mousse (Solero)	1 serving	193	2	14	15	67	54	19	1
Marsala & Mascarpone Zabaglione (Damian's)	1 serving	282	5	32	14	44	241	77	3
Mashed Sweet Potatoes with Garlic (Lancaster)	1 serving	201	2	21	13	56	16	787	2
*Modified Recipe	1 serving	127	2	21	4	31	5	11	2
Mixed Berry Cobbler (Redwood)	1 serving	534	4	84	22	36	64	127	3
*Modified Recipe	1 serving	517	5	85	19	32	52	125	3
Molasses & Honey Roasted Pork Tenderloin (Mark's)	1/4 recipe	660	50	59	25	34	142	312	1
*Modified Recipe	1/6 recipe	394	33	40	11	26	93	98	1
Mussel Soup (Cavatore)	1 serving	879	63	70	35	37	127	1401	3
*Modified Recipe	1 serving	723	56	70	22	27	113	817	3
Oatmeal Custard (Brennan's)	1 serving	323	8	43	14	38	170	83	2
*Modified Recipe	1 serving	310	9	43	12	34	37	113	2
Oven Baked Salmon on Rock Salt (Clive's)	8oz fillet	337	43	0	17	48	136	103	0
*Modified Recipe	6oz fillet	253	32	0	13	48	102	77	0
*Pico de Gallo Rice (Houstonian)	1/2 cup	130	3	26	2	11	0	446	1
*Modified Recipe	1/2 cup	130	3	26	2	11	0	23	1

	Portion	Calories	Protein (g)	Carbohydrate (g)	Fat (g)	% Fat Calories	Cholesterol (mg)	Sodium (mg)	Dietary Fiber (g)
Pork Loin with Perfumes (Arcodoro)	1/6 recipe	638	51	48	25	36	134	424	5
*Modified Recipe	1/8 recipe	464	38	36	17	33	101	318	4
Red Onion Marmalade (Riviera)	2 tablespoon	39	0	3	3	71	5	24	0
*Modified Recipe	2 tablespoon	16	0	3	1	27	1	24	0
Red Pepper Bisque with Tabbouleh (Bistro Lancaster)	1 serving	215	4	21	14	54	27	1196	4
*Modified Recipe	1 serving	141	5	21	6	32	13	8	4
Roasted Duck with Cherry Sauce (La Tour)	1/2 duck	1762	88	23	142	73	398	279	0
*Modified Recipe	1/4 duck, no skin	350	32	12	18	46	126	91	0
Roasted Flounder with Garlic & Bacon (Chez Nous)	1 serving	1119	100	23	69	56	367	1125	5
*Modified Recipe	1 serving	839	96	23	39	42	283	970	5
Roasted Red Bell Pepper Soup (Solero)	1 serving	281	3	12	26	79	82	742	2
*Modified Recipe	1 serving	126	7	18	4	26	2	212	2
Roasted Sweet Garlic Whipped Potatoes (DeVille)	1 serving	427	7	48	23	49	8	87	3
*Modified Recipe	1 serving	327	7	48	12	33	5	87	3
Root Vegetable Slaw with Vinaigrette (Brennan's)	1 serving	170	2	8	16	78	0	49	2
*Modified Recipe	1 serving	104	2	7	8	66	0	49	2
*Salmon de Coquina (La Tour)	1 serving	390	48	22	13	29	106	133	4
Salmon Risotto with Cream Sauce (Grille 5115)	1 serving	902	54	48	53	53	245	598	4
*Modified Recipe	1 serving	649	54	46	26	37	156	262	4
Sauteed Shrimp with Hot Sauce (Ambassador)	1 serving	217	25	14	7	28	172	1187	1
*Modified Recipe	1 serving	217	25	14	7	28	172	282	1
Scalloped Potatoes (Riviera)	1 serving	578	15	43	40	61	134	385	3
*Modified Recipe	1 serving	340	15	48	10	27	32	315	3
Seared Sea Scallops with Marmalade (Riviera)	1 serving	139	6	7	10	65	27	209	1
*Modified Recipe	1 serving	67	6	7	2	26	12	209	1
Shelly's Salad with Pecans (Redwood)	1 serving	432	10	27	34	67	6	487	3
*Modified Recipe	1 serving	257	4	23	18	60	6	133	3
Shrimp Arturo (Solero)	1/2 recipe	1600	45	144	90	50	246	695	8
*Modified Recipe	1/4 recipe	574	23	73	20	31	64	349	4
Shrimp Giuliana (Cavatore)	1 serving	310	9	14	24	68	121	73	1
*Modified Recipe with rice	1 serving	413	13	59	13	28	90	73	2
Shrimp Orzo Ferrari (La Tour)	1 serving	896	27	103	43	42	46	605	7
*Modified Recipe	1 serving	711	27	103	22	27	46	472	7
Shrimp with Frangelico Sauce (Aldo's)	1 serving	623	7	42	43	61	70	131	2
*Modified Recipe	1 serving	408	7	42	18	40	32	132	2
Snapper Escabeche (Solero)	1 serving	458	36	10	30	60	63	127	2
*Modified Recipe	1 serving	279	36	10	10	33	63	127	2
Southern Star Chocolate Cake (Aldo's)	1 serving	768	13	70	45	51	264	380	4
Southwest Caesar Salad (Houstonian)	1 serving	771	18	32	65	75	79	2195	8
*Modified Recipe	1 serving	235	11	23	12	45	17	375	8

	Portion	Calories	Protein (g)	Carbohydrate (g)	Fat (g)	% Fat Calories	Cholesterol (mg)	Sodium (mg)	Dietary Fiber (g)
*Southwest Pasta Primavera (Rice)	1 serving	642	21	105	15	21	5	132	7
Steak of Gold (Arcodoro)	16-oz ribeye	907	94	2	53	54	269	234	0
*Modified Recipe	6-oz tenderloin	291	36	2	13	40	106	81	0
Steamed Salmon with Ginger & Scallions (Empress)	1 serving	291	43	2	11	35	111	1458	0
*Modified Recipe	1 serving	291	43	2	11	35	111	234	0
Sticky Toffee Cake with Sauce (Clive's)	1 serving	623	5	94	27	38	142	259	2
*Modified Recipe	1 serving	448	5	78	14	28	72	254	2
Stilton, Greens with Walnuts & Vinaigrette (Riviera)	1 serving	576	11	6	58	89	33	497	3
*Modified Recipe	1 serving	173	4	4	17	83	8	84	3
Stuffed Mushroom with Sauce & Relish (Café Noche)	1 serving	475	17	17	38	70	107	483	4
*Modified Recipe	1 serving	137	10	15	6	34	19	280	4
Stuffed Pork Loin (Damian's)	1 serving	1474	103	30	104	64	431	2488	4
*Modified Recipe	1 serving	455	44	22	22	43	184	240	4
Susan's Mother's Carrot Cake & Frosting (Grille 5115)	1/8 recipe	1188	11	157	60	44	246	823	3
*Tabbouleh (Bistro)	1/2 cup	67	2	11	3	31	0	7	2
*Modified Recipe	1/2 cup	47	2	11	0	5	0	7	2
*Tahitian Vanilla Fruit Soup (DeVille)	1 serving	388	1	99	0	1	0	2	3
Texas Crab Cakes with Soy Ginger Butter (DeVille)	1 serving	472	25	16	35	64	74	750	4
*Modified Recipe	1 serving	245	24	14	11	38	50	501	4
Texas Pecan Chocolate Torte/Anglaise (Epicurean)	1/8 recipe	762	10	73	50	57	210	180	2
*Modified Recipe	1/12 recipe	508	6	48	33	59	140	120	2
Thai Sticky Rice with Custard (Nit Noi)	1 serving	678	12	106	24	32	106	348	5
Thomas Salad with Dressing (Damian's)	1 serving	524	26	35	31	54	70	1253	4
*Modified Recipe	1 serving	254	9	31	11	39	8	415	3
Three Milk Cake (Café Noche)	1/8 recipe	1141	27	133	57	45	524	599	1
Tiramisu (Arcodoro)	1/6 recipe	699	13	70	36	46	417	274	1
Twice Baked Potatoes (Mark's)	1 serving	341	11	28	21	55	58	212	4
*Modified Recipe	1 serving	197	6	27	8	34	23	88	4
Upside-down Apple Tart (Rotisserie)	1/6 recipe	1001	7	124	56	49	180	20	5
Veal Marsala (Cavatore)	1 serving	650	26	34	45	61	154	1602	1
*Modified Recipe	1 serving	396	26	22	22	49	118	584	1
Vegetable Ragout with Chervil (Chez Nous)	1/6 recipe	136	2	6	12	77	31	25	2
*Modified Recipe	1/6 recipe	47	2	6	2	38	5	24	2
Venison Tenderloin with Peppers (Rotisserie)	1 serving	1112	58	28	86	69	322	1533	6
*Modified Recipe	1 serving	565	52	28	27	43	188	635	6
Walnut Tart with Jack Daniel's Ice Cream (Chez Nous)	1 serving	1116	14	99	73	57	278	467	2
Warm Croissant Bread Pudding (Bistro Lancaster)	1 serving	1206	13	129	70	52	470	1062	3
White Chocolate Ice Cream Charlotte (St. Regis)	1 serving	1434	35	184	63	39	974	314	2
White Gazpacho (Chez Nous)	1 serving	331	5	14	29	78	0	31	3

INDEX

ALDO'S 13

AMBASSADOR 17

Appetizers

Ceviche Solero (Solero) 114

Ceviche with Avocado Cream Sauce
(Café Noche) 40

Fried Calamari (Cavatore) 44

Gougères (DeVille).............................62

Stuffed Mushroom Appetizer, White
Wine Butter Sauce, Corn Relish
(Café Noche) 38

ARCODORO 23

Berkman, Clive (Clive's) 53

BISTRO LANCASTER 27

Boada, Arturo (Solero) 111

Bread

Cornmeal Drop Biscuits, Beef Debris
Gumbo with (Brennan's) 35

Jalapeño Corn Muffins
(Redwood Grill) 100

Brennan-Martin, Alex (Brennan's) 33

BRENNAN'S...33

Butera, Joseph A. "Bubba" (Damian's) .57

CAFÉ NOCHE 37

CAVATORE 43

Cavatore, Giancarlo
(Cavatore, La Tour d'Argent).......43, 79

CHEZ NOUS..47

Clive's...53

Chen, Scott (Empress) 65

Cox, Mark (Mark's)..............................83

DAMIAN'S..57

Dash, Charles (St. Regis) 115

Desserts

Baked Alaska (Post Oak Grill)...........96

Chocolate Molten Soufflé with White
Chocolate Sauce (Brennan's) 36

Crème Brûlée Riviera (Riviera Grill)..104

Lemon Baked Cheesecake (Empress).68

Macadamia Nut Chocolate Caramel
Torte (The Houstonian) 78

Mango Mousse (Solero)....................114

Marsala and Mascarpone Zabaglione
with Strawberries (Damian's)..........60

Mixed Berry Cobbler (Redwood Grill) 100

Oatmeal Custard (Brennan's).............36

Sticky Toffee Cake with Caramel
Sauce (Clive's) 56

Susan's Mother's Carrot Cake with Cream
Cheese Frosting (Grille 5115) 74

Tahitian Vanilla Fruit Soup (DeVille) ..64

Texas Pecan Chocolate Bourbon Torte
with Bourbon Crème Anglaise
(Epicurean Catering Company).....122

Thai Sticky Rice with Thai Custard
and Mango (Nit Noi) 92

The Southern Star (White or Dark
Chocolate Cake) Southern Star Sauce
(Aldo's)..16

Three Milk Cake (Café Noche) 39

Tiramisu (Arcodoro)...........................26

Upside-down Caramelized Apple Tart,
Pastry Dough (Rotisserie for Beef and
Bird) 110

Walnut Tart with Jack Daniel's Ice
Cream (Chez Nous) 49

Warm Croissant Bread Pudding, Mulled
Sultanas, Rum Vanilla Bean Caramel
Sauce (Bistro Lancaster) 30

White Chocolate Ice Cream Charlotte
(St. Regis)......................................118

DeVILLE 61

Drought, Shelly (Redwood Grill) 97

EMPRESS 65

Fish and Seafood

Corn Crusted Redfish With Cilantro
Avocado Sauce (Post Oak Grill) 95

Fried Calamari (Cavatore) 44

Roasted Flounder with Garlic & Bacon
(Chez Nous) 48

Salmon

Cedar Planked Salmon with Raspberry
Chipotle Sauce (Epicurean Catering
Company)......................................120

Oven Baked Salmon on Rock Salt
(Clive's)...54

Salmon de Coquina, Coquina Salsa
(La Tour d'Argent) 81

Salmon Risotto with Red Pepper Cream
Sauce (Grille 5115).........................73

Steamed Salmon with Fresh Ginger
(Empress)...67

Seared Sea Scallops with Red Onion
Marmalade (Riviera Grill) 102

Shrimp

Ceviche Solero (Solero) 114

Ceviche with Avocado Cream Sauce
(Café Noche) 40

Chilled Jumbo Shrimp with Jalapeño
Remoulade (Redwood Grill)...........99

Grilled Shrimp with Tomato Jam
(Epicurean Catering Company).....121

Jalapeño Barbequed Shrimp with Pico
de Gallo Rice (The Houstonian) 77

Sautéed Shrimp with Hot Sauce
(Ambassador) 18

Shrimp Arturo (Solero) 113

Shrimp Giuliana (Cavatore) 45

Shrimp with Frangelico Sauce (Aldo's).14

Shrimp Orzo Ferrari (La Tour d'Argent)...80

Snapper
Crispy Red Snapper (Nit Noi) 91
Fillet of Snapper with Roasted Garlic
Sauce (Aldo's) 15
Snapper Escabeche (Solero) 113
Texas Gulf Coast Lump Crab Cakes,
Ginger Soy Butter (DeVille) 63
Fisher, Ethel (Post Oak Grill,
Redwood Grill) 93, 97
GRILLE 5115 71
THE HOUSTONIAN 75
Jachmich, Manfred (Post Oak Grill,
Redwood Grill) 93, 97
Lahham, Sonny (Cavatore, La Tour
d'Argent) 43, 79
LA TOUR d'ARGENT 79
Malla, Hessni (La Tour d'Argent).........79
Mallett, Alan (Café Noche) 37
Mandola, Frank B. (Damian's)..............57
Mannke, Joe (Rotisserie for
Beef and Bird) 107
MARK'S..83

Meat

Beef
Braised Beef with Brown Sauce
(Ambassador) 20
Filet Mignon a la Empress (Empress) .66
Grilled Angus Filet Mignon with
Mushroom, Dried Cranberry Ragout
(Riviera Grill) 103
Steak of Gold (Arcodoro) 24

Lamb
Lamb Enchiladas, Enchilada Sauce
(Post Oak Grill) 94
Lamb Shanks Osso Buco Style (Aldo's) .15

Pork
Grilled Pork Chops with Pecan Sauce
(Bistro Lancaster)............................29
Honey Crimson Glazed Pork
Tenderloin, Mixed Greens, Toasted
Pecans (Epicurean Catering
Company)..121
Molasses and Honey Roasted Pork
Tenderloin, Caramelized Balsamic
Vinegar Sauce (Mark's) 86
Pork Loin with Perfumes of the Forest
with Tarragon Blueberry Sauce
(Arcodoro) 25
Stuffed Pork Loin, Marinade, Spinach
Stuffing, Mushroom Topping
(Damian's) 59
Veal Marsala (Cavatore) 46

Venison
Herb Seared Axis Venison and Pinot
Noir Sauce (St. Regis)....................116
Venison Tenderloin with Bell Peppers
(Rotisserie for Beef and Bird)........109
Mills, Jim (The Houstonian) 75

Miscellaneous
Candied Pecans, Shelly's Salad, Honey
Balsamic Vinaigrette with (Redwood
Grill)..98
Green Enchiladas, Tomatillo Sauce
(Café Noche) 39
Mulled Sultanas with Warm Croissant
Bread Pudding and Rum Vanilla Bean
Caramel Sauce (Bistro Lancaster) ...30
Red Onion Marmalade, Seared Sea
Scallops with (Riviera Grill)..........103
Sirloin and Ribeye Rub (Clive's)........55

Spicy Walnuts, Stilton, Endive and
Baby Field Greens, Walnut
Vinaigrette with (Riviera Grill).....102
Steak Cooking Tips (Clive's)............55
NIT NOI 89

Pasta, Rice
Corn Risotto (Mark's) 85
Dominic's Penne Pasta (Damian's).....60
Fettuccine Roma (Cavatore).............46
Pico de Gallo Rice, Jalapeño Barbequed
Shrimp with (The Houstonian)......77
Shrimp Orzo Ferrari (La Tour d'Argent)..80
Southwestern Pasta Primavera
(Epicurean Catering Company).....120
Thai Sticky Rice with Thai Custard and
Mango (Nit Noi)............................92
Piper, Melissa (Brennan's)..................105
POST OAK GRILL 93

Poultry
Alice's Chicken Delight (Nit Noi).....90
Chicken Griselda (La Tour d'Argent)...81
Chicken Grogorio (Cavatore)...........45
Chicken with Dry Red Peppers
(Ambassador) 19
Crispy Chicken with Ginger, Green
Onion Sauce (Empress)...................67
Mallard Duck with Black Walnuts
(Rotisserie for Beef and Bird)........108
Roasted Duck with Cherry Sauce
(La Tour d'Argent) 82
REDWOOD GRILL 97
RIVIERA GRILL 101
ROTISSERIE FOR BEEF AND BIRD..107
Sadler, Bill 37
St. Regis..115

Salads, Dressings

Dijon Vinaigrette (Clive's) 56

Field Greens and Artichoke Salad,
Vinaigrette (Arcodoro) 24

Goat Cheese Salad, Apple and
Sun-Dried Tomato Vinaigrette
(Grille 5115) 72

Root Vegetable Slaw, Ginger
Vinaigrette (Brennan's) 35

Shelly's Salad, Candied Pecans, Honey
Balsamic Vinaigrette (Redwood Grill) ..98

Stilton, Endive and Baby Field Greens,
Spicy Walnuts, Walnut Vinaigrette
(Riviera Grill) 102

Southwest Caesar Salad, Spicy Caesar
Dressing (The Houstonian) 76

Tabbouleh, Red Pepper Bisque with Lump
Crabmeat and (Bistro Lancaster) 28

Thomas' Salad, Dressing (Damian's) ..58

Sauces and Salsas

Avocado Cream Sauce, Ceviche with
(Café Noche) 40

Bourbon Crème Anglaise, Texas Pecan
Chocolate Bourbon Torte with
(Epicurean Catering Company) 122

Caramelized Balsamic Vinegar Sauce,
Molasses and Honey Roasted Pork
Tenderloin with (Mark's) 86

Caramel Sauce, Sticky Toffee Cake
with (Clive's) 56

Cherry Sauce, Roasted Duck with
(La Tour d'Argent) 82

Cilantro Avocado Sauce, Corn Crusted
Redfish with (Post Oak Grill) 95

Coquina Salsa, Salmon de Coquina
with (La Tour d'Argent) 81

Enchilada Sauce, Lamb Enchiladas
with (Post Oak Grill) 94

Jalapeño Remoulade, Chilled Jumbo
Shrimp with (Redwood Grill) 99

Pinot Noir Sauce, Herb Seared Axis
Venison with (St. Regis) 117

Red Pepper Cream Sauce, Salmon
Risotto with (Grille 5115) 73

Rum Vanilla Bean Caramel Sauce, Warm
Croissant Bread Pudding, Mulled
Sultanas, with (Bistro Lancaster) 30

Southern Star Sauce, The Southern
Star (White or Dark Chocolate
Cake), with (Aldo's) 16

Tarragon Blueberry Sauce, Pork Loin
with Perfumes of the Forest, with
(Arcodoro) 25

Tomatillo Sauce, Green Enchiladas
with (Café Noche) 39

White Chocolate Sauce, Chocolate
Molten Soufflé with (Brennan's) 36

Sheely, John and Alicia (Riviera Grill) ...101

SOLERO 111

Soup

Beef Debris Gumbo, Creole Brown
Roux (Brennan's) 34

Beer Cheese Soup (Redwood Grill) ...99

Bread Soup (Aldo's) 14

Cabbage Soup (Nit Noi) 91

Champagne Brie Soup en Croute
(St. Regis) 112

Grilled Corn Chowder with Red
Potatoes and Thyme (Mark's) 84

Lentil Soup (La Tour d'Argent) 80

Mussel Soup (Cavatore) 44

Red Pepper Bisque with Lump
Crabmeat & Tabbouleh (Bistro
Lancaster) 28

Roasted Red Bell Pepper Soup
(Solero) 116

Tahitian Vanilla Fruit Soup (DeVille) 64

White Gazpacho (Chez Nous) 48

RICE EPICUREAN MARKETS /
EPICUREAN CATERING
COMPANY 119

SHOPPING GUIDE 130

SPECIAL HELPS 128

Torres, Greg (Cavatore) 43

Vegetables

Black Truffle Whipped Potatoes (St.
Regis) 117

Charred Vegetable Plate (Solero) 113

Creamed Spinach (Clive's) 54

Eggplant Szechwan Style (Ambassador).19

Mashed Sweet Potatoes with Roasted
Garlic (Bistro Lancaster) 29

Roasted Sweet Garlic Whipped
Potatoes (DeVille) 64

Scalloped Potatoes Riviera
(Riviera Grill) 104

Twice Baked Potatoes (Mark's) 85

Vegetable Ragout with Chervil
(Chez Nous) 50

Walker, Carl (Brennan's) 33

WHO'S WHO

Key to Back Cover Photograph

1 **Ann Criswell,** *Author*
2 **Fran Fauntleroy,** *Publisher*
3 **Ann Steiner,** *Editor*
4 **Polo Becerra,** *Post Oak Grill*
5 **Charles Dash,** *St. Regis*
6 **Tommy Leman,** *Damian's*
7 **Louis Cressy,** *Bistro Lancaster*
8 **Shelly Drought,** *Redwood Grill*
9 **Melissa Piper,** *Brennan's*
10 **Carl Walker,** *Brennan's*

11 **Arturo Boada,** *Solero*
12 **Scott Chen,** *Empress*
13 **Wendy Wang,** *Ambassador*
14 **Jim Mills,** *The Houstonian*
15 **Aldo ElSharif,** *Aldo's*
16 **Alice Vongvisith,** *Nit Noi*
17 **Stephan Gasaway,** *Chez Nous*
18 **Joe Mannke,** *Rotisserie for Beef and Bird*
19 **John Sheely,** *Riviera Grill*

20 **Hessni Malla,** *La Tour d'Argent*
21 **Alan Mallett,** *Café Noche*
22 **Mark Cox,** *Mark's*
23 **Frederic Perrier,** *Grille 5115*
24 **Tim Keating, DeVille,** *Four Seasons*
25 **Efisio Farris,** *Arcodoro*
26 **Gregory Torres,** *Cavatore*
27 **Linda McDonald,** *Nutritionist*
28 **Napoleon Palacios,** *Damian's*